Praise for
THE ESSENTIAL JEWEL
OF HOLY PRACTICE

"Here, translated into very accessible English, beautifully presented in a spacious edition appropriate to the expansive Dzogchen doctrine, is Patrul Rinpoche's summary of the path of integrated practice for an authentic compassionate practitioner. It is a moving and transcendent vision of Buddhism uniting wisdom, care for others, and mantra."

—GARETH SPARHAM,
translator of *Vast as the Heavens, Deep as the Sea*

"Patrul Rinpoche's *Essential Jewel* is a treasure trove packed with wisdom and skillful means for all levels of Buddhist practice. Garfield and McRae here offer a fresh translation of Patrul's song of instruction, presented in a bilingual format and accompanied by their novel, Madhyamaka-inspired interpretation of the nature and origins of Vajrayana and Dzogchen. The blessings of the six-beat mantra are sure to bring awakening in our hearts!"

—THOMAS DOCTOR,
research scholar, Rangjung Yeshe Institute

"A beautiful and lucid translation of a textual gem by one of Tibet's most eloquent teachers. This work offers advice on how to live in the world and cultivate our best potential in light of Buddhist ethics and philosophy."

—JANET GYATSO,
Hershey Professor of Buddhist Studies, Harvard University

The Essential Jewel of Holy Practice

Patrul Rinpoche

Introduction,
translation, and commentary by

JAY L. GARFIELD

EMILY W. MCRAE

Wisdom Publications
199 Elm Street
Somerville, MA 02144 USA
wisdompubs.org

Library of Congress Cataloging-in-Publication Data
Names: O-rgyan-jigs-med-chos-kyi-dbang-po, Dpal-sprul, 1808–1887, author. | Garfield, Jay L., 1955– translator, writer of added commentary. | McRae, Emily W. translator, writer of added commentary.
Title: The essential jewel of holy practice / Patrul Rinpoche; introduction, translation, and commentary by Jay L. Garfield, Emily W. McRae.
Other titles: Thog mtha' bar gsum du dge ba'i gtam lta sgom spyod gsum nyams len dam pa'i snying nor. English
Description: Somerville, MA: Wisdom Publications, 2017. | Includes bibliographical references and index. | Translated from Tibetan. | Identifiers: LCCN 2017027247 (print) | LCCN 2017032331 (ebook) | ISBN 9781614294634 (ebook) | ISBN 1614294631 (ebook) | ISBN 9781614294474 (paperback) | ISBN 161429447X (paperback)
Subjects: LCSH: Rdzogs-chen. | BISAC: RELIGION / Buddhism / Tibetan. | RELIGION / Eastern. | RELIGION / Ethics.
Classification: LCC BQ7662.4 (ebook) | LCC BQ7662.4 .O72913 2017 (print) | DDC 294.3/923—dc23
LC record available at https://lccn.loc.gov/2017027247

ISBN 978-1-61429-447-4   ebook ISBN 978-1-61429-463-4
21 20 19 18 17
5 4 3 2 1

Cover design by Graciela Galup. Cover image: Avalokiteśvara, from the private collection of Jay Garfield. Photo by Stephen Petegorsky. Interior design by Gopa&Ted2. Set in Diacritical Garamond Pro 11/15 and Qomolangma Title 13/23.

Wisdom Publications' books are printed on acid-free paper and meet the guidelines for permanence and durability of the Production Guidelines for Book Longevity of the Council on Library Resources.

♻ This book was produced with environmental mindfulness. For more information, please visit wisdompubs.org/wisdom-environment.

Printed in the United States of America.

MIX
Paper from
responsible sources
FSC
www.fsc.org   FSC® C011935

Please visit fscus.org.

We dedicate this translation to
all of the Tibetan teachers
who have kept the Buddhadharma and the
great Tibetan lineages alive,
both under occupation and in exile.

Contents

His Holiness the Dalai Lama

Dza Patrul Rinpoche was a humble monk and erudite scholar who dedicated himself to practicing what is taught in Śāntideva's *How to Lead an Awakened Life* (*Bodhicaryāvatāra*), the transmission and explanation of which I received in this lineage from Khunu Lama Rinpoche. The essential point of it is that we need to transform ourselves in thought, word, and deed, which requires mindfulness, introspection, and conscientiousness.

His *Essential Jewel of Holy Practice*, which I like for its direct, down-to-earth style, was explained to me by Dilgo Khyentse Rinpoche. It begins with a salutation to the Three Jewels. It touches on how to turn away from the preoccupations of this life. It explains how to overcome the misconception of self and alludes to guru yoga in stating that the ultimate lama is the innate mind of clear light. It mentions that some Mādhyamikas allow that things have some objective existence, whereas the Prāsaṅgika Mādhyamikas state that although there is appeareance, there is no independent objective existence whatever. The text goes on to distinguish the views of sutra and tantra as being differentiated not in terms of their object but in terms of the subjective perspective. Lines close to the end summarize the teaching—"If you examine your mind continuously, whatever you do, you are following the perfect path."

I congratulate Jay Garfield and Emily McRae on making this fresh English translation in which they have tried to reflect the simple but profound meaning of Patrul Rinpoche's advice. It will appeal especially to readers who seek a succinct rendition of all the essential instructions of the bodhisattva path.

The Dalai Lama

INTRODUCTION TO

The Essential Jewel of Holy Practice
by Patrul Rinpoche

JAY L. GARFIELD, EMILY W. MCRAE

PATRUL RINPOCHE

Orgyen Jigme Chokyi Wangpo, better known as Patrul Rinpoche, was one of the most influential philosophers and meditation masters of nineteenth-century Tibet. He was an adept
of the Dzogchen (Great Perfection) tradition associated with
the Nyingma school and a scholar of both Madhyamaka philosophy and tantra. Patrul Rinpoche is the author of many
influential and widely read texts, including his classic introduction to and synopsis of the Buddhist path, *The Words of
My Perfect Teacher*.[1] He was also renowned as a meditator and
Dzogchen practitioner.

Patrul Rinpoche's prose and poetry is profound, philo-
sophically precise, eloquent, and yet completely accessible to

1. Patrul Rinpoche, *The Words of My Perfect Teacher*, trans. Padmakara
Translation Group (Boston: Shambhala Publications, 1998).

advanced scholars and practitioners as well as to laypeople and novices. As one of his disciples noted, even if his teachings "are heard by a dull mind, still they are easy to understand" (Thondup, 209).[2] The text we present here, *The Essential Jewel of Holy Practice*, conveys in lucid and evocative poetry the subtlest aspects of the phenomenology of liberation and the relationship between Buddhist philosophical tenets, the practice of the path to awakening, and the cultivation of moral sensitivity. Patrul Rinpoche speaks directly and powerfully, but intimately, to the reader without alienating her; the intimacy he achieves only enhances the reader's connection to the text. Another great Dzogchen master of that time, the third Dodrupchen, wrote: "Patrul uses fearful and overwhelmingly tough words, but there is no trace of hatred or attachment in them. If you know how to listen to them, they are directly or indirectly only teachings. Whatever he says is solid like gold—it is true" (Thondup, 208).

Patrul Rinpoche was born in eastern Tibet in 1808. His spiritual biography (in the hagiographic style characteristic of this Tibetan genre) reports that he chanted the syllable *oṃ* immediately after he was born and clearly recited the full Avalokiteśvara mantra—*oṃ maṇi padme hūṃ*—when he was only five days old. This mantra, to which he refers in the present text as the "six-beat mantra" (*yig drug*), had special significance for Patrul Rinpoche. Most Tibetans believe that reciting this mantra develops the attitude of universal care

2. Tulku Thondup, *Masters of Meditation and Miracles*, ed. Harold Talbott (Boston: Shambhala Publications, 1999).

embodied by the celestial bodhisattva Avalokiteśvara. Patrul Rinpoche is credited with disseminating the practice of regularly reciting this mantra, and hence with emphasizing the importance of the cultivation of an attitude of care in daily practice among the laypeople of eastern Tibet. The advice to "chant the six-beat mantra" is repeated over twenty times in *The Essential Jewel of Holy Practice*. The associated development of an altruistic attitude of universal care (*karuṇā*) and the aspiration to attain awakening for the benefit of all beings (*bodhicitta*) was at the heart of many of Patrul Rinpoche's teachings. One of his daily practices was to chant Śāntideva's *How to Lead an Awakened Life* (*Bodhicaryāvatāra*), a text that he taught frequently and on which he composed an influential commentary.

Patrul Rinpoche was a Dzogchen master. In the Dzogchen tradition, the recognition of the nature of mind requires the assistance of a teacher who will "indicate" or introduce the disciple to the nature of her own mind. Sometimes these "indication" instructions employ unconventional methods, as in Patrul Rinpoche's case. According to his biography, one day when Patrul Rinpoche was meditating in his hermitage, one of his root teachers, Do Khyentse, visited him. When Patrul Rinpoche went out to greet him, Do Khyentse grabbed him by the hair and dragged him around. Patrul Rinpoche smelled alcohol on Do Khyentse's breath and thought, "The Buddha expounded on the dangers of alcohol, yet even a great adept like him could get drunk like this" (Thondup, 202). Do Khyentse immediately released Patrul Rinpoche and spat in his face, shouting, "Alas, that you intellectual people have such evil thoughts! You old dog!" Patrul Rinpoche was astounded by both his own negative thoughts and his teacher's clairvoyance. In that moment, it is reported that Patrul Rinpoche "meditated on the enlightened nature of his mind, and a clear, sky-like, open and intrinsic awareness awakened in him." He realized, in other words, the nature of his own mind. In honor of this event, Patrul Rinpoche jokingly took Old Dog as his spiritual name.

Many of Patrul Rinpoche's students were impressed by his honesty and humility. It is said that when he died, his sole possessions were one set of robes, an alms bowl, a yellow shawl, a lower garment, some food, and a few books. He collected so few possessions while alive that "wherever he was, when he stood up, he was ready to leave a place instantly" (Thondup, 209). Patrul Rinpoche did not store offerings that were made to him—except for a few days' worth of food—and often left them in the place they were made. As a result, he was often followed by a band of poor people, the best beneficiaries of the offerings.

Because of his simple, coarse dress and his utter lack of pomp, people often failed to recognize him as a great lama. In fact, one well-meaning monk, not knowing it was him, once gave Patrul Rinpoche a teaching on one of Patrul Rinpoche's own compositions! The third Dodrupchen remembered Patrul Rinpoche as treating "all people equally, neither flattering them in their presence nor backbiting them in their absence. He never pretends to be something or someone else . . . He is not partial to high people, nor does he have any disregard for ordinary people . . . He seems hard to serve, yet however close you are to him, it is impossible to find a single instance of dishonesty, dubiousness, instability, or hypocrisy in him." Despite Patrul Rinpoche's exacting moral standards, Dodrupchen also describes him as relaxed and easy to be around. He inspires such devotion and affection that "it is hard to separate from him" (Thondup, 208).

At the age of eighty, Patrul Rinpoche's health declined. On the eighteenth of the fourth month of the fire-pig year (1887), he sat naked in Buddha posture. Eyes open in meditative gaze, his "mind merged into the primordial purity" and he died soon after. The impact of his life was great, not only because of his scholarly and poetic achievements but also because of the powerful example he set and the fierce compassion he modeled.

The Essential Jewel

In the colophon, Patrul Rinpoche tells us that *The Essential Jewel of Holy Practice* was written in the White Cliff Victory Mountain Cave (near the Chinese-Tibet border) in response to "the pleas of an old friend." The poem discusses the perils of ordinary life in samsara and the urgency of cultivating moral and spiritual discipline in order to escape samsara and benefit oneself and others. The text offers a succinct, yet complete, view of the path of liberation as seen from the perspectives of Madhyamaka philosophy and Mahāyāna ethics refracted through Dzogchen. Our translation and explanatory notes emphasize the ways in which Patrul Rinpoche integrates the Madhyamaka understanding of emptiness and the Mahāyāna ideal of compassionate care with the Dzogchen perspective, yielding a sophisticated philosophical approach to meditative practice focusing on the nature of the experience both of emptiness and of liberation.

Dzogchen is a tradition of Tibetan Buddhism principally associated with the Nyingma (ancient, or original) school. According to the Nyingma tradition, Dzogchen teachings were first introduced in Tibet in the eighth century with the arrival of Padmasambhava, the Indian tantrika, who, along with the scholar Śāntarakṣita, brought Buddhism from India to Tibet. Padmasambhava himself is regarded by many Tibetans as a buddha. There does not seem, however, to be textual evidence of Dzogchen in early Indian Buddhist texts—the earliest known Dzogchen texts are in Tibetan and from the tenth century—and many scholars of Dzogchen consider it to be a uniquely Tibetan religious tradition. The greatest expounder of Dzogchen philosophy and practice was Longchen Rabjam (1308–1364), who, it is said, transmitted the central Dzogchen teachings *The Heart Essence of the Great Expanse* (*Klong chen nying thig*), four centuries later, to Jigme Lingpa (1730–1798). These teachings were the basis of Patrul Rinpoche's classic text *The Words of My Perfect Teacher*.

Dzogchen, in Tibetan, is an abbreviation of *rdzogs pa chen po*, which literally means "the great perfection." Perfection, according to Dzogchen, is not something we need to produce, achieve, or even cultivate; it is innate in each of us, and the goal of practice is simply to recognize it. In this context, "perfection" is understood to denote *buddha nature*, the qualities and capacities of a buddha that are already complete and latent within us. According to Dzogchen—and this is what differentiates it from other Buddhist traditions that share its emphasis on buddha nature—this recognition is best achieved by a simple, direct realization of the nature of one's own mind (*rig pa*).

This realization is normally achieved in the context of meditation, which, in the Dzogchen tradition, is not the attainment of fixed concentration or single-pointed focus but rather the cultivation of open, nondistracted awareness. When we rest in this open awareness, Dzogchen practitioners say, we find that grounding every moment of consciousness, no matter how conceptual—and therefore necessarily distorting—is a basic, luminous, nondual awareness. Dzogchen practitioners are therefore encouraged to relax into this basic awareness, allowing their thoughts and feelings to arise and to cease. Therefore Dzogchen teachers such as Patrul Rinpoche often call on us to give up our frenetic activity and simply to relax. The language of naturalness, relaxation, and spontaneity is central to Dzogchen teachings, including Patrul Rinpoche's, since our main obstacle to liberation, they say, is the habit of busying and distracting the mind and thereby failing to recognize its natural purity and power.

One of the main themes of the *Essential Jewel* is that any mental state or activity—from perception and sensation to thought and emotion—can "self-liberate" (*rang grol*) on its own as it arises. He advises, "Leave things in their natural state. Don't fabricate and clarity will arise on its own" (v. 39). This, we might say, is because the essence of mind—empty awareness—is already primordially liberated. The path to liberation is not a gradual cultivation of qualities one lacks, but rather a quest to recognize and to manifest the liberation already present. If we are able to reconnect with our mind and our being as it is, and to develop the stability to rest in that experience, there is nothing further that needs to be done to uproot affliction or confusion; if we persist in trying to change our own nature, we only erect obstacles to liberation. As Patrul Rinpoche puts it, "Only by doing nothing can we do all there is to be done" (v. 39).

The Dzogchen tradition distinguishes four aspects of liberation, each of which is articulated in the *Essential Jewel*: (1) primordial liberation (*ye grol*), (2) self-liberation (*rang grol*), (3) naked liberation (*cer grol*), and (4) instant liberation (*shar grol*).[3] To understand the *Essential Jewel* one must have a sense of each of these aspects of liberation. The attainment of awakening in this framework necessarily exemplifies all four aspects.[4]

We have alluded to primordial liberation, the fact that all mental experiences are already liberated because they are empty of intrinsic nature. The contemporary Buddhist teacher Dzogchen Ponlop Rinpoche writes that, for any experience we may have, "we do not need to re-create that ground of emptiness, because it is already there" (108). Whatever it

---

3. Lexically, *liberation upon arising*; the property of a thing being liberated the moment it arises.

4. These four modes of liberation are discussed in Longchenpa's *sNying thig ya bzhi*, vol. 12 (*Zab mo yang thig*), 152b–153a. For a contemporary discussion, see Dzogchen Ponlop Rinpoche, *Mind Beyond Death* (Ithaca, NY: Snow Lion Publications, 2008), 108–10.

is that we are experiencing—thought, perception, emotion, etc.—is not essentially afflicted, simply because it has no essence whatsoever. No state of mind has any intrinsic nature, and so each is already empty, with its emptiness always available for realization. In the context of Dzogchen philosophy of mind, primordial liberation is just this emptiness of mental experience.

Self-liberation, which Patrul Rinpoche discusses at length in the *Essential Jewel*, is the fact that afflicted experience can become liberation without the aid of anything external to it, "like a snake that simply uncoils itself from its own knot" (Dzogchen Ponlop, 108). This is true in the relative sense, since afflictive experiences, like all conditioned phenomena, are impermanent and so will cease; we do not have to do anything to make them impermanent. But this is true in a deeper sense: Our thoughts, emotions, and perceptions are themselves displays of the nature of mind, which is primordially liberated. By simply recognizing their primordial nature, we can become liberated from attachment to them and from the experience of our mind as intrinsically existent. This is self-liberation: because they are primordially liberated, afflictive experiences can self-liberate.

The third aspect of liberation is naked liberation, which is the liberation that occurs by virtue of the mind becoming aware of itself. Patrul Rinpoche describes this mode of liberation when he advises us not to pursue the object of our afflictive thoughts and emotions but instead to attend to the afflicted mind (vv. 50–54). This kind of attention to the mind is called "naked" because it is attention that is not dressed up with concepts and narratives, or concerned with the contents of mind, as opposed to the mind itself; it is called "liberation" because the very activity of attending in this way liberates afflictive experience, transforming what was a source of suffering into a source of liberation simply by freely attending to it rather than being bound by it. We achieve instant liberation, the fourth and final mode of Dzogchen liberation, when we continue, moment after moment, to allow afflictive experience to liberate us and thus become able to rest stably in the nature of our mind, which we come to experience as nondual and boundless.

Patrul Rinpoche's discussion of the liberation of affliction and the recognition of the basic nature of mind (*rig pa*) is grounded in the core Mahāyāna philosophical tenets of emptiness (*śūnyatā, stong pa snyid*) and compassionate care (*karuṇā, snying rje*). According to the Madhyamaka school, all phenomena are ultimately empty, which means that they lack any intrinsic existence. This is true of physical objects, persons, mental states, and even emptiness itself. Although they exist in a conventional sense, upon analysis we find that they have no intrinsic reality. On the Madhyamaka view, this emptiness of intrinsic reality needs to be understood intellectually, through philosophical analysis, and, more important, to be deeply and stably integrated into our experience, leading to a constant, immediate experience of the fundamental nature of reality.

It is easy to read nihilism into Madhyamaka texts by mistakenly taking the claim that all phenomena are empty of intrinsic existence to mean that nothing at all exists. But to experience the world as a Mādhyamika is not to experience things as nonexistent; in fact, this kind of nihilism is a danger all Buddhist schools admonish us to avoid. Instead, emptiness is offered as a philosophical analysis of the *way in which things exist*—they exist only conventionally—and not as a denial that they exist at all. To exist conventionally is to exist as posited in the framework of human thought, language, and conceptual structures; it is to be causally and mereologically interdependent, and to be dependent for identity on conceptual imputation. This kind of existence, Mādhyamikas argue, is the only existence there is; there is no deeper, ultimate existence.

It is important to remember that, for Mādhyamikas, things exist conventionally *because* they lack intrinsic existence, and not in spite of this fact. Emptiness and dependent origination —the idea that phenomena exist dependent on conditions— are identified in Madhyamaka philosophy, as argued by the second-century philosopher Nāgārjuna in his classic treatise *Fundamental Verses on the Middle Way*. In that text, Nāgārjuna argues that there is no ontological distinction between the two truths: samsara and nirvana are identical; conventional and ultimate truth are merely two sides of the same coin. This identification of the two truths and the doctrine that even emptiness is empty—not an alternative reality standing behind an illusory conventional reality—undermines any nihilistic interpretation of emptiness in Madhyamaka philosophy. Our goal, according to this tradition, is to experience the empirical reality of phenomena and their ultimate emptiness simultaneously. As Patrul Rinpoche says many times in the *Essential Jewel*, all phenomena, including the self, are simply "empty appearances"—they are empty, but they are still appearances.

To experience *ourselves* in this way is an enormous conceptual and phenomenological challenge, for even when we seem to be able to take external phenomena to be empty of essence, interdependent, impermanent, and selfless, we often do so by implicitly taking ourselves to be the intrinsic ground of that mere imputation. No matter what we think about external phenomena, there is still a powerful cognitive instinct to take ourselves as the foundation of our experience; denying our own intrinsic existence seems, then, like cognitive suicide—like the denial of the reality of the very subject performing the denial. But it is not. It is simply to realize that we as subjects, like the objects we experience, exist only in interdependence and have an identity that is only conceptually imputed. To see subjectivity itself not as the primordial ground of reality but as one more groundless reality is the goal of a Madhyamaka understanding; the transformation of consciousness this realization entails is so profound as to be literally inconceivable until it has been achieved.

Following the Dzogchen tradition, Patrul Rinpoche argues that to understand emptiness is to realize directly the emptiness of one's own mind and mental constructs. "Your mind, nondually aware and empty," Patrul Rinpoche tells us, "is the embodiment of truth" (v. 39). The *Essential Jewel* can be understood as deep personal instruction in recognizing the empty nature of one's own mind (*rig pa*). In this text, Patrul Rinpoche often uses more phenomenological descriptions of emptiness, referring to clear, naked, nondual, empty awareness. These expressions characterize the *experience* of emptiness as opposed to emptiness itself. According to Patrul Rinpoche, because the nature of mind is empty, if we recognize that basic nature, we've recognized emptiness, and if we achieve a stable recognition of the nature of mind, we thereby achieve a stable understanding of emptiness. To understand the nature of mind, then, is to understand the nature of reality.

To understand the nature of mind as clear, open, luminous, empty awareness is therefore radically transformative, and this transformation extends to one's moral capacity and sensitivity. Recognizing the nature of mind allows our dysfunctional mental states to self-liberate: when we recognize the emptiness of our mental states, our attachment to them simply disappears. These dysfunctional states, which include confusion, aversion, attraction, and envy, are major obstacles to loving and compassionate care for other sentient beings. For this reason, the Dzogchen imperative to rest in the nature of one's mind has profound moral power, since this way of being in the world allows one to spontaneously manifest the Mahāyāna commitment to care for all beings with love and compassion (*karuṇā*).

Our innate dysfunctional states cause, maintain, and are maintained by egocentrism, which inhibits a more realistic, wholesome, productive mode of interpersonal experience and interaction. When we are in the grip of such states, not only do we fail to generate any love or compassion, but the love and compassion that we may already have can't be utilized; for our loving care to be actualized it can't be blocked, warped, or hijacked by egocentricity. A mind in which this kind of primal confusion and dysfunction does not take hold is a mind that can be sensitive to the needs to others and that can care for them. One of the major lessons of the *Essential Jewel* is that the recognition of the nature of mind is a moral accomplishment, a fact that is further emphasized by Patrul Rinpoche's repeated encouragement to recite the six-beat mantra, the mantra of universal care.

As the focus on the six-beat mantra suggests, the *Essential Jewel* is as much about practice as it is about philosophy. But the practices recommended in this text are subtle, especially compared with the Mahāyāna and Vajrāyāna practices described in Patrul Rinpoche's other works, including *The Words of My Perfect Teacher* and his commentary on the *Bodhicaryāvatāra*, which advocate practices ranging from radical generosity to complex visualizations. These ethical practices are not at odds with those suggested in the *Essential Jewel*. (Indeed, Patrul Rinpoche most likely assumed at least some of them as a context for the text.) But they are not explicitly thematized here.

Instead, the *Essential Jewel* focuses on more subtle shifts of attention and mental orientation from the outside to the inside, from objective phenomena to the structure of subjectivity—for instance, the shift from attending to the object of our envy to attending to our own envious mind (v. 53), or the shift from taking for granted the reality of our confused thoughts to recognizing our own confusion (v. 54). These reorientations from the object to the subject side of experience have radical consequences, since they allow our states of mind to self-liberate.

After explaining the Dzogchen view of liberation, Patrul Rinpoche concludes the *Essential Jewel* with the heartfelt plea to put the view into practice. The practice he envisions involves changing our usual priorities, taking the goal of achieving liberation to be paramount and recognizing the relative triviality of most of our other concerns. It also involves rewriting our narratives about our own lives, accepting our roles as agents of our own suffering and as potential agents of our own liberation. Patrul Rinpoche argues that if we really understand this text, we should be motivated to undertake this radical transformation.

Radical transformation sounds hard and the reader may wonder if such a demand is reasonable. Patrul Rinpoche asks such a reader, "Where have your habits and activities gotten you so far?" (vv. 65–71). Not to awakening, clearly. To motivate the radical change that the path to liberation requires, Patrul Rinpoche relies on a common argument in Buddhist ethical texts: Although we know that death is certain, the time and manner of our own death is uncertain. So we must do what is important—practice the Dharma—in the precious time that we have left in our human bodies: "There is no time! No time! No time to spare! When the Lord of Death suddenly arrives, what can you do? Right now, and from now on, please practice the divine Dharma. Right now, with haste, chant the six-beat mantra" (v. 72).

Notes on the Translation

We approach the *Essential Jewel* both as a masterpiece connecting Madhyamaka and Dzogchen philosophy to practice and as a brilliant and moving piece of poetry. In Tibetan,

Patrul Rinpoche's verses are alive with evocative metaphor, alliteration, and rhythm. But unlike much Buddhist philosophical poetry, he eschews classical ornament, technical terminology, and elaborate construction. His language is direct and colloquial; the beauty of his poetry is its simplicity and intimacy. Nonetheless, the poem is marked by recurrent poetical devices. We have therefore tried to translate this more as a poem than as a precise philosophical treatise, sometimes sacrificing lexical precision in favor of poetic device. This seems appropriate, as Patrul Rinpoche himself has clearly opted for poetics over precision in many places. (On the other hand, Patrul Rinpoche does sometimes explicitly employ technical vocabulary from Buddhist philosophical and Dzogchen traditions. Where he does so, we have kept our translation precise, reflecting that technical vocabulary, sometimes at the cost of poetic felicity.)

It is impossible when translating in this way to transpose Tibetan poetic devices directly into English; the languages, the syllabic structure, and the prosody are just too different. Instead, we have used English poetic devices that are structural analogues of those Patrul Rinpoche deploys in Tibetan. We have attempted to convey as much as possible of the earthy beauty of the original by preserving alliteration whenever possible, providing an English cadence that does in English what the Tibetan cadence does in Tibetan. We have kept notes to a minimum, providing what we hope is enough to make apparent to the English reader what would be apparent to Patrul Rinpoche's Tibetan audience, but allowing the poem to speak as directly as Patrul Rinpoche intended it.

Thanks to Pema Tenzin for help tracing the names of Avalokiteśvara. We thank Thomas Doctor, Douglas Duckworth, and Sonam Thakchöe for extensive and careful comments on an earlier draft of this translation. They each corrected errors and suggested more elegant formulations than we had found. Thanks also to You Jeen Ha, Halley Haruta, and Emma Taussig for extensive editorial assistance and many useful suggestions regarding the notes and translation. We thank Blaine Garson and Surya Pierce for helpful critique, and Asha Pierce for teaching us to cultivate patience in the final preparation of this manuscript. This translation is much better for their assistance. Any errors that remain are our own; we are keenly aware of the shortcomings in our own understanding of the ideas Patrul Rinpoche explores.

ཐོག་མཐའ་བར་གསུམ་དུ་དགེ་བའི་གཏམ་ལྷ་སྐྱེམ་སྐྱོང་གསུམ།

ཉམས་ལེན་དམ་པའི་སྐྱིང་རོར་ཞེས་བྱ་བ་ཞུགས་སོ།།

དཔལ་སྤྲུལ་རིན་པོ་ཆེ།།

The Essential Jewel of Holy Practice:

A Discourse Virtuous in the Beginning, Middle, and End on the View, Meditation, and Action

by Patrul Rinpoche

༄༅། །གན་མོ་ལོ་ཀ། ཤ་ར་ཡ།

༡

གང་མཚན་བདུད་རྩིའི་ཟེགས་མ་བཅིག་ལྷུང་བས།།

ཚོ་རབས་དུ་མར་རྐ་བར་ཚོས་ཀྱི་སྒྲས།།

འབྱེངས་པའི་ངོ་མཚར་རིན་ཆེན་རྣམ་གསུམ་ཞེས།།

གྲགས་པའི་དཔལ་ནེས་ཀུན་དུ་ཞིས་བྱུར་ཅིག།

Homage to Avalokiteśvara!

I.

May the glorious fame of the Triple Gem—
just by the sound of Dharma in their ears,
or even a single drop of the nectar of his name—
bring good fortune to all for countless lives.

VERSES 1–3

These first three verses are purely introductory. They establish an intimate voice that persists through the poem. The name to which Patrul Rinpoche refers in verse 1 is that of Avalokiteśvara, as is clear from the homage. Avalokiteśvara is the embodiment of universal care (*karuṇā*) and plays a central role in Patrul Rinpoche's account of practice.

༢

གང་ཞིག་སྟོན་ཀྱི་དུས་ན་ཨ་སྲའི་འབྲས།།

ཁ་ཚིག་ནང་མ་སྨིན་ཀྱང་ཕྱི་སྨིན་འདྲ།།

སྙང་བ་དེ་ལྟར་ཚོས་པའི་གཟུགས་བརྣན་བདག།

སེམས་དང་ཚོས་མ་འདྲེས་ཕྱིར་ཚོས་གཏུམ་དགོན།།

༣

དེ་ལྟར་ན་ཡང་དམ་པ་ཁྱེད་ཀྱི་བཀའ།།

བསྐུལ་བའི་ནན་མ་སྤོག་ཕྱིར་དུང་པོའི་ང།།

སྲིགས་སྟོང་ཕལ་བའི་ཆུལ་དང་མི་མཐུན་པར།།

གཡོ་སྒྱུ་མེད་པའི་སེམས་ཀྱིས་གསོལ་འདིར་དགོངས།།

2.

Like a mango in the autumn that appears ripe from without,
but is green within, I have but a semblance of virtue.
So my advice may be inept:
my mind is still not one with the Dharma.

3.

Nonetheless, I can't disobey your command.
Since I will speak the truth—a rare thing in this dark,
degenerate time—please try to understand all
I tell you and be firm and resolute in purpose.

ༀ

དང་སྲོང་ཆེན་པོ་ཐུབ་དབང་ལྷའི་ཡང་ལྕུས།།

དང་པོའི་ལམ་ནས་དང་པོའི་གོ་འཕང་བརྙེས།།

དང་པོའི་ལམ་བཟང་འགྲོ་ལ་དང་པོར་སྟོན།།

དེ་ལྟར་དང་སྲོང་ཆེ་ཞེས་གྲགས་མིན་ནམ།།

༤

ཀྱེ་མ་སྐྱེ་བགས་མའི་དུས་འདིར་འགྲོ་བའི་རྒྱུད།།

དང་པོའི་གཞུང་བཟང་ཉམས་ནས་གཡོ་སྒྱུ་སྟོང་།།

དེ་ལྟར་འཁྲུག་པའི་སྐྱོ་དང་འཁྲུག་པོའི་དག།

བུ་སྲུས་གཉེན་སེམས་བསྐྱ་ལ་སུ་ཡིད་གཏོད།།

Verse 4

This verse indicates the close connection that Patrul Rinpoche will establish between the correct view and the path to virtue and liberation. It is common to regard knowledge and understanding to be prerequisites for effective practice; Patrul Rinpoche argues instead that firm practice is necessary in order to cultivate proper understanding.

4.

The magnificent sage, the Buddha, the god of gods,
attained a straight understanding by following the
straight path, and honestly showed that straight path to
    other beings.
Isn't this the reason he is known as the true sage?

5.

Woe to beings in this impure age! They have turned from
the straight, honest path of the Dharma to perversity.
And so, with crooked thought and crooked speech,
they lead others' minds astray. Who can you rely on?

Patrul Rinpoche repeats the Tibetan term *drang* six times in this verse. We
have generally translated it as "straight," as opposed to "correct," but it also
connotes honesty and truth. To keep the English clean we've had to use the
terms "honest" and "true" to translate two occurrences of *drang*, thus sacrificing some of the power Patrul Rinpoche achieves through repetition.

ཀྱི་དུད་སྤྲིགས་འགྲོ་མཐོང་ནས་སྟོ་འདི་ལྟོང་ས༎

ཀྱི་མ་སུ་ཡི་ངག་ལ་སུ་ཡིད་རྟོན༎

མི་སྟུན་སྲིན་པོའི་སྐྱིང་ན་གནས་འདུ་འདི༎

དགོངས་ནས་རང་རྟིན་རང་ལ་ཆེ་བར་མཛོད༎

སྤྲིན་ཡང་རང་སེམས་རྩལ་ཤེས་གཅིག་པུ་ཞིག༎

འབྲམས་ཤིང་ལས་ཀྱིས་བདས་ནས་འདིར་སྐྱེར་ཟིན༎

ད་ཡང་མར་གྱི་དཀྱིལ་ནས་སུ་བཏོན་ལྟར༎

ཐམས་ཅད་བཞག་ནས་རང་ཞིང་གཅིག་པུར་འགྲོ༎

6.

How sad! To see such degenerate beings is so depressing!
Woe to all of us! You can't trust anybody.
It's like living in the land of man-eating demons.
So do yourself a big favor and take my point!

7.

Although it is embodied now, your consciousness
took rebirth here impelled by karma from another realm.
Nonetheless, just like a hair drawn from butter,
you will surely depart alone, leaving everything behind.

༩

རང་སེམས་རང་ལ་མི་དཀར་ཐབས་མེད་ཀྱིས།།

རང་བློ་རང་ལ་མི་དྲང་མི་སྲིད་ཀྱིས།།

རང་དོན་སྙིང་པོའི་ལྷ་ཆོས་མ་འགྲུབ་ན།།

རང་སྲིད་རང་གིས་བཀྲག་པ་མ་ཡིན་ནམ།།

༡༠

སྲིབས་པའི་སྐྱེ་བོ་བསམ་སྦྱོང་དཔན་ཆེས་བས།།

སུས་ཀྱང་རང་ལ་མི་ཕན་གཡོ་སྒྱུས་བསྐུ།།

སུ་ལ་འང་རང་གིས་ཕན་པ་འགྲུབ་དཀའ་བས།།

འདུ་འཛིའི་འཁྲུལ་ཐག་བཅད་ན་མི་ལེགས་སམ།།

VERSES 9–10

These might appear a bit shocking in the context of the bodhisattva path that enjoins the cultivation of bodhicitta—the aspiration to liberation for the benefit of all beings—as it appears that Patrul Rinpoche is suggesting that we simply disregard others. But this is not the point. Instead, he is arguing that we can't be of any use to others at all until we have achieved a

8.

Granted, we are unable to perfect ourselves,
but it still makes no sense to neglect our minds.
Aren't we just throwing away our precious lives
when we fail to engage in Dharma practice?

9.

Ordinary people are so degraded.
Their vicious thoughts and actions do no good for
    themselves or others.
And they are deceitful. What can you do for them?
Wouldn't it be best to withdraw from all of this?

reasonably high level of realization, and that doing so requires that we first isolate ourselves from the distractions of social life and from the pernicious effects of ingratitude and harassment. After all, if we wish to become good doctors so as to cure disease, we must first withdraw from ordinary society and devote ourselves to medical study.

༡༠

བཀུར་ཀྱང་གོང་མ་མཉེས་དུས་མི་འོང་གིས།།

སྐྱོང་ཡང་འོག་མ་མག་དུས་མི་འོང་གིས།།

བརྩེ་ཡང་པར་བསམ་ཆུར་ལ་མི་སེམས་པའི།།

ཆུལ་འདི་དགོངས་ལ་བློ་ཐག་ཆོད་པར་མཛོད།།

༡༡

མཁས་ཀྱང་བསྐུན་དོན་མི་འགྲུབ་ཆོད་པ་འཕེལ།།

གྲུབ་ཀྱང་གནན་དོན་མི་འབྱུང་བློ་སྐྱུར་མང་།།

མཐོ་ཡང་སྡེ་ཆུས་མི་འོང་ཞེངས་ཕོག་ཆེ།།

ང་ལྟའི་དུས་འདི་དགོངས་ལ་སྐྱོ་བར་མཛོད།།

10.

You can't please exalted people, even by honor.
You can't please common people, even by nurture.
Nobody ever even returns your affection.
Think about this and make a firm commitment.

11.

Learning doesn't lead to progress, only to disputes.
Achievement doesn't help others, they only run it down.
Status doesn't help the country, it only sparks revolt.
So when you gaze on this dark age, feel only sorrow.

༡༢

བཕད་ཀྱང་བདེན་དུ་མི་འཛིན་གཞན་དུ་གོ །
ཕན་སེམས་གཏིང་ནས་དཀར་ཀྱང་ལོག་པར་འཛིན། །
འཁྲུག་པོས་དྲང་པོ་འཁྲུག་པོར་མཐོང་དུས་འདིར། །
སུ་ལའང་ཕན་པ་མི་འགྱུར་རེ་ཐག་ཆོད། །

༡༣

ཚོས་ཀུན་སྐུ་མ་ལྟུ་བུར་རྒྱལ་བས་གསུངས། །
དངེ་སྐུ་མ་ལས་ཀྱང་སྐུ་ཆེན་ཏེ། །
གཡོ་སྐུའི་སྐུ་མ་ཆོས་པའི་མིག་འཕྲུལ་མཁན། །
སྲིབས་སྟོང་སྐུ་མ་འདི་ལ་འཇིགས་པར་མཛོད། །

12.

Even if you explain, people will misunderstand you.
Even pure motivation is regarded as base.
These days, the perverse see the truth as perversion.
So who can you help? Nobody. Abandon all hope!

13.

The Victor says that all things are illusion-like.
But even among illusions, there are greater illusions!
Deceitful illusions wrought by shifty magicians!
Beware of all these crafty, slimy illusions!

Verse 13

The "greater illusions" to which Patrul Rinpoche refers in verse 13 are the
tendencies he discusses in verse 12: to misunderstand Dharma explana-
tions, to regard pure motivation as base, and to see truth as perversion.

གཏུམ་རྣམས་བྲག་ཙ་སྤྲ་བུར་རྒྱལ་བས་གསུངས།།

དངི་བྲག་ཙ་ལས་ཀྱང་ཡང་ཙ་སྟེ།།

ཁ་དང་དོན་དུ་མི་མཚུངས་བྲག་ཙའི་གཏུག།

སྤྲ་ཚིག་བྲག་ཙ་འདི་ལ་སྨན་པ་སྐྱེད།།

སུ་མཐོང་མི་མ་ལགས་ཏེ་སྤྲུ་བྱེད་མཁན།།

སུས་བཏགས་གཏམ་མ་ལགས་ཏེ་བསྐུ་བྱེད་ཚིག།

དངི་སུ་ལའང་བློ་གཏད་མི་འདུག་གིས།།

རང་ཉིད་གཅིག་པུ་རང་དགར་གནས་པར་མཛོད།།

14.

The great masters have said that all our speech is but
    an echo.
But even among echoes, there are re-echoes!
People never say what they mean.
Their echoic speech is deceptive, so enough of these echoes!

15.

Nobody is authentic anymore; they're all just impostors.
They utter not authentic speech but deceptive lies.
Who can you trust? Absolutely no one. So, go!
Always live alone and keep your independence!

ཕུས་སྐྱོད་ཚོས་བཞིན་སྐྱོད་ན་ཀུན་དང་འགའལ།།

ངག་གཏམ་དྲང་པོར་བཤད་ན་ཕལ་ཆེར་ཁྲོ།།

སེམས་བཟང་གཏིང་ནས་དགར་ཀྱང་སྐྱོན་དུ་རྩི།།

དངི་རང་ཚུལ་སྐྱེད་པའི་དུས་ལ་བབ།།

ཕུས་སྤུས་དབེན་པའི་རི་ལ་གཅིག་པུར་སྡོད།།

ངག་སྤུས་སྒྲ་བ་མ་མང་འཁྱིལ་ཐག་ཆོད།།

སེམས་སྤུས་རང་སྐྱོན་ཁོ་ནར་ཅེར་རེ་ལྟོས།།

སྤུས་པའི་རྣལ་འབྱོར་ཟེར་ན་དེ་ལ་ཟེར།།

16.

Even if your acts conform to Dharma, you will be at odds
   with the world.
Even if you speak the truth, people will be angry.
Even if you are always kind and pure, they will find fault.
So from now on, please, just keep your words and actions
   secret.

17.

Conceal your body by living alone on a desolate mountain.
Conceal your speech by cutting off all contact and saying
   but little.
Conceal your mind by attending carefully to each of your
   own faults.
This is what it takes to be a concealed practitioner.

༡༨

སུ་ལ་འང་རྫོ་གཏད་མི་འདུག་ཞེ་ལོག་གོ །

གང་ལ་འང་སྙིང་པོ་མི་འདུག་སྐྱོ་ཆད་དེ །

གང་བསམ་འགྲུབ་དུས་མི་འདུག་ཐད་ཐག་ཆོད །

འདི་གསུམ་གཏན་དུ་འགྲོགས་ན་ཕན་པར་མཆིས །།

༡༩

སྐྱིད་དུས་མི་འདུག་སྐྱིད་པོ་ད་ནི་ཟད །

ཕུག་པོ་མི་འདོད་ཕྱུག་མཐའ་ཆོས་ཀྱིས་ཆོད །

སྐྱིད་ཕྱུག་ཅི་ཡོང་སྟོན་ལས་བཙན་པོས་ཉེས །།

ད་ནི་སུ་ལ་འང་མི་རེ་མི་དོགས་སོ །།

VERSES 18–19

Here Patrul Rinpoche introduces some nice psychological paradoxes: revulsion (*zhe log*) and despondency (*skyo ched*) are paired with resolution (*thag chod*); happiness (*skyid*) and suffering (*sdug*) are equally presented as impermanent. But revulsion and despondency with the world of suffering

18.

Maintain revulsion—nobody can be trusted.
Maintain despondency—nothing has any substance.
Stay resolute—there's no time for all your plans.
These three attitudes will make you useful.

19.

There's no time for happiness; it just disappears.
No one wants suffering; cut it off through Dharma.
All happiness or suffering is governed by karma.
So please place neither hope nor doubt in anyone.

are meant to be goads, inspiring resolution to withdraw from suffering and to overcome it. The impermanence of happiness in samsara is one more reason to transcend samsara itself, thus eliminating all suffering, leading to the permanent happiness of liberation.

མི་ལ་རེ་ཆེ་རེ་ཁ་འཇོམ་སྒུལ་སྒུལ།།

རང་ལ་དགོས་མང་དགོས་དགོས་སྐྱབ་པའི་ཐོས་མས།།

འདི་བྱུ་འདི་བྱེད་བྱི་ཚོས་རེ་དོགས་སྦྲོ།།

ད་ནི་ཅི་ལ་བབ་ཀྱང་མི་བྱེད་དོ།།

བསྐྱེད་རིམ་རྣམ་གྲངས་མང་མང་སྦྲོ་མི་འཆུད།།

ལོ་བཀུར་བསྒྲུད་ཀྱང་མི་དགའལ་ཡང་ཚོ་སོང་།།

ད་ནི་ཕྱི་ཡང་གསོན་ཡང་ཚོ་འདིས་ཅི།།

ཕྱི་མའི་ཚོས་ཚམ་འགྲུབ་ན་དེ་ག་རང་།།

20.

Placing hope in everyone you meet, you greet them
  with a smile;
with so many demands, you are always running about:
first do this, then do that, torn between your hopes
  and doubts!
From now on, no matter what you face, stop acting
  like that!

21.

Even if you die today, do not grieve—that's the way of
  samsara.
Even if you live to be one hundred, don't rejoice—
  youth will be long gone.
What does it matter if you live or die right now—
  what good is this life, anyway?
So, for your own sake, just practice Dharma from now on.

༢༢

ཀྱི་མ་བདག་གི་མགོན་གཅིག་ཕྱགས་རྗེའི་གཏེར།།
རྩ་བའི་བླ་མ་མགོན་པོ་སྤྱན་རས་གཟིགས།།
གསུང་གི་སྙིང་པོ་དྲུ་ཚོས་ཡི་གེ་དྲུག།
དྭ་ཉི་རེ་ས་ཁྱེད་ལས་མི་འདུག་གོ།

༢༣

ཤེས་ཚད་གོ་བར་ལྷུས་ནས་ད་མ་པན།།
བྱས་ཚད་ཚེ་འདིར་ཕྱིར་ནས་ད་མ་པན།།
བསམ་ཚད་འཁྲུལ་པས་སོང་བས་ད་མ་པན།།
ཡིན་དེས་ཡིག་དྲུག་བསྒྲང་བའི་དུས་ལ་བབ།།

VERSES 22–25

At this point, Patrul Rinpoche introduces Avalokiteśvara, the celestial bodhisattva who is the embodiment of universal care (*karuṇā, snying rje*) and the six-beat mantra (*yig drug*), *oṃ maṇi padme hūṃ*. Patrul Rinpoche will insist from here that the cultivation of an attitude of care is the preeminent requirement for practice and cultivation. Nothing else matters if

22.

Avalokiteśvara is your sole protector and guardian,
the great treasury of compassion, your foundation lama!
The essence of his speech, the holy Dharma, is the six-beat
    mantra.
From this time forth, he is your only source of hope!

23.

Nothing good has come from your useless knowledge.
Nothing good has come from working for this life.
Nothing good has come from your delusional thinking.
Now is the time to do some good: Chant the six-beat
    mantra.

our attitude to the world is not one of care; if we cultivate care, everything
else follows.

The repeated, mantra-like admonition to "chant the six-beat mantra"
(*yig drug sgrongs*) is not, as it might appear, a recommendation to engage

མི་བསྐུལ་གཏན་གྱི་སྐྱབས་གཅིག་དགོན་མཆོག་གསུམ།།

དགོན་མཆོག་ཀུན་འདུས་རྡོ་རྗེ་སློབ་དཔོན་ལ་ཟིགས།།

ཁྱེད་ཤེས་བློ་གཏད་གཅིག་ལས་མི་འགྱུར་བའི།།

ཟེར་ཤེས་བློ་ཕུགས་ཆོད་ལ་ཡིག་དྲུག་སྟོང་ས།།

ཐེག་ཆེན་ལམ་གྱི་རྩ་བ་བྱང་ཆུབ་སེམས།།

སེམས་མཆོག་རྒྱལ་བ་ཀུན་གྱི་བགྲོད་གཅིག་ལམ།།

ལམ་བཟང་བྱང་ཆུབ་སེམས་དང་མི་འབྲལ་ཞིང་།།

འགྲོ་ལ་སྙིང་རྗེའི་དང་ནས་ཡིག་དྲུག་སྟོང་ས།།

in mindless ritual chanting, but rather a metonym. Mantra recitation is undertaken in order to directly transform the mind. Recitation of the Avalokiteśvara mantra is taken in the Tibetan tradition to lead the practitioner to become more caring. Patrul Rinpoche, in most of the

24.

The only firm, nondeceptive refuge is the Triple Gem.
The sole embodiment of the Triple Gem is Avalokiteśvara.
With unwavering, steadfast confidence in his wisdom,
with certainty and resolution, chant the six-beat mantra.

25.

Bodhicitta is the sole foundation of the Mahāyāna path.
This is the aspiration of every moral hero.
Never leaving the high road of bodhicitta,
with compassion for all beings, chant the six-beat mantra.

remainder of the poem, therefore advises us to do whatever is necessary
to re-create ourselves as more caring individuals and to locate the goal of
self-reconstruction at the center of our practice.

ཐོག་མེད་འཁོར་བར་འཁྱམས་ནས་ད་ཕན་ཆད༎
ཅི་བྱེད་སྡིག་ཏུ་སོང་ནས་སྡིག་པར་འཁྱམས༎
སྡིག་ལྔང་སྡིང་ནས་མཐོལ་ཞིང་བཤགས་སེམས་ཀྱིས༎
སྡོམས་བཞི་ཚང་བའི་དད་ནས་ཡིག་དྲུག་སྒྲོངས༎

Verses 26–28

In these three verses, Patrul Rinpoche connects self-grasping—the view that one is an independent ego—to vice and suffering, and liberation to the cultivation of care. When we take ourselves to be independent egos, we draw the essential distinction between self and other, and we each place ourselves at the center of our own universe and regard others as existing merely as our objects. That is not only irrational but also leads to the attraction and aversion that generate suffering. An attitude of care allows us to eradicate that self-grasping and to liberate ourselves and others from suffering.

Verse 26: The four capacities (*stobs bzhi*) to be cultivated are the capacity of stability (*rten gyi stobs*), the capacity of remorse (*rnam par sun 'byin pa'i*

26.

Wandering in samsara from beginningless time,
all your acts are vicious, so you keep roaming through
    more rebirths.
From the depths of your heart, renounce your vices.
Endowed with the four capacities, chant the six-beat mantra.

stobs), the capacity of renunciation of wrongdoing (*nyes pa las slar ldog pa'i stobs*), and the capacity of counteracting that wrongdoing (*gnyen po kun tu spyod pa'i stobs*). These are enumerated in Patrul Rinpoche's *The Words of My Perfect Teacher* (*Kun bzang bla ma'i zhal lung*).

We first cultivate a stability of purpose that allows us to engage in the psychological work of self-transformation. We then consider our faults and cultivate genuine remorse for them. Based on that remorse, we renounce that wrongdoing. Finally, we lead a life that counteracts the effects of that wrongdoing, and in which it is impossible to return to our previous state of vice. Here Patrul Rinpoche emphasizes that the entire process is a manisfestation of the attitude of care.

༣༠

བདག་འཛིན་ཞེན་པའི་སྐྲོ་འདི་སྤྱིད་པའི་རྒྱུ།།

དེ་སྐྱེད་ལུས་དང་ལོངས་སྤྱོད་དགེ་བའི་ཚོགས།།

ཡར་མཆོད་མར་སྤྱིན་འབོར་དས་ཀུན་ལ་བསྒོ།།

གཅེས་འཛིན་རྒྱངས་ཀྱིས་སྐྱུར་ལ་ཡིག་དྲུག་སྒྲོངས།།

༣༡

སངས་རྒྱས་ཀུན་གྱི་ངོ་བོ་བླ་མ་རྗེ།།

སྐུ་དྲིན་སངས་རྒྱས་ཀུན་ལས་ལྷག་པའི་མགོན།།

བླ་མ་སྐྱུན་རས་གཟིགས་དང་དབྱེར་མེད་དུ།།

དད་པའི་གདུང་ཤུགས་སྐྱེད་ལ་ཡིག་དྲུག་སྒྲོངས།།

48

27.

Your obsessive self-grasping mind only perpetuates samsara.
So give everything—your body, your possessions, and your
    virtue—
to those above and to those below, to all in samsara and all in
    nirvana,
and casting off attachment, chant the six-beat mantra.

28.

Your exalted teacher has the nature of all the buddhas,
and of all the buddhas, he is the kindest.
Since the teacher is inseparable from Avalokiteśvara,
with great devotion, chant the six-beat mantra.

སྒྲིབ་བྱང་ལས་སློབ་སྐུ་བཞི་མངོན་དུ་བྱེད།།
དབང་བཞིའི་བདག་ཉིད་བླ་མ་སྒྲུབ་རས་གཟིགས།།
རང་སེམས་བླ་མར་ཤེས་ན་དབང་བཞི་རྫོགས།།
རང་དབང་རང་ཐོབ་རང་ནས་ཡིག་དྲུག་སྒྲོང་།།

VERSE 29

The four embodiments of buddhahood are: (1) the physical embodiment (*nirmāṇakāya, sprul pa'i sku*), (2) the embodiment as enjoyment (*sambhogakāya, long spyod dzogs pa'i sku*), (3) the embodiment as the manifestation of reality (*dharmakāya, chos kyi sku*), and (4) the embodiment as the nature of buddhahood (*svabhāvikakāya, ngo bo nyid skyi sku*). (It is more common to talk about three embodiments of buddhahood; the fourth is usually introduced in tantric contexts.) To embody buddhahood, or full awakening, in one's material life (*nirmāṇakāya*) is to manifest one's awakening in one's physical actions and appearance. To embody full awakening in enjoyment (*sambhogakāya*) is to manifest freedom from suffering and joyful engagement with the world. To embody awakening as a manifestation of reality (*dharmakāya*) is for one's speech and thought to represent the world as it is, not illusion. To embody awakening as the nature of buddhahood (*svabhāvikakāya*) is for one's buddha nature to be constantly manifested, requiring no further causes and conditions, thus demonstrating that it is one's very essence (*svabhāva, ngo bo nyid*).

29.

Clearing the fog, practicing the path, achieve the four
    embodiments!
Avalokiteśvara has the nature of the four empowerments.
When you realize your mind as your teacher, they are all
    achieved.
So, having achieved innate empowerment, chant the
    six-beat mantra.

The four empowerments (*dbang bzhi*) are: (1) the vase empowerment
(*bum pa'i dbang*), (2) the secret empowerment (*gsang pa'i dbang*), (3) the
knowledge-wisdom empowerment (*shes rab ye shes kyi dbang*), and (4) the
precious word empowerment (*tshig dbang rin po che*). The vase empowerment purifies the accumulated karma from the negative actions of the
body, the secret empowerment purifies the karma from negative speech,
the knowledge-wisdom empowerment purifies the karma from negative
mental actions, and the precious word empowerment purifies all cognitive
obscurations. These empowerments are the basis of most tantric initia-
tions, including those in the Dzogchen tradition.

Patrul Rinpoche also introduces the idea of the mind as a teacher. The
intention of this phrase is that by realizing the nature of mind through the
kinds of contemplation facilitated by the four empowerments, the practitioner comes to understand the nature of mind itself, the nature of suffering, and the path to its elimination.

འཆོར་བ་རང་སྲུང་ཚམ་སྟེ་ལོགས་ན་མེད།།

སྲུང་ཕྱིད་ལྟ་ར་ཤེས་ན་གཞན་དོན་རྟོགས།།

དག་སྲུང་དབང་བཞི་འགྲོ་ལ་དུས་གཅིག་བསྐུར།།

འཆོར་བ་དོང་སྤྲུགས་རང་རས་ཡིག་དྲུག་སྦྱོངས།།

30.

Samsara is mere appearance, nothing more.

See mundane appearance as divine to benefit others.

By seeing things this way, you grant all beings the four
empowerments.

Plumbing the depths of samsara, chant the six-beat mantra.

In these verses Patrul Rinpoche emphasizes the identity of the conventional and the ultimate. Samsara and nirvana are identified, with samsara understood only as an illusory appearance of the world of liberation, and nirvana taken to be that world understood as it is. Also note that that in verses 31–33 Patrul Rinpoche moves from acts of mind to acts of speech to acts of body, gradually bringing understanding into mundane activity, which will be the topic of the next section of the poem.

༣༠

བསྐྱེད་རིམ་རྣམ་གྲངས་མང་པོ་སྟོ་མི་འབྲུ།།

བདེ་གཤེགས་གཉིས་བསྐྱོམ་རྒྱལ་བ་ཀུན་ཀྱི་ངང་།།

གང་སྣང་སྣང་བ་ཕྱགས་རྗེ་ཆེན་པོའི་ཀླ།།

སྣང་སྟོང་ལྷ་སྐུའི་དང་ནས་ཡིག་དྲུག་སྒྲོངས།།

༣༡

བསྒྲེས་བརྗོད་བསྙེན་སྒྲུབ་ལས་སྤྱགས་སྤྲོས་པ་ཚམ།།

ཆིག་ཚོང་ཡི་གེ་དྲུག་པ་ཚམས་ཀྱི་ཀླ།།

སྒྲ་གྲགས་འཐབས་པའི་གཤུང་དང་འདུ་འབྲལ་མེད།།

གྲགས་སྟོང་སྤྲགས་སུ་ཤེས་པས་ཡིག་དྲུག་སྒྲོངས།།

31.

Your mind cannot hold the vast array of visualizations.
To meditate on one tathāgata is to meditate on all the
    masters.
Whatever appears is the embodiment of great compassion.
In the divine embodiment of appearance and emptiness,
    chant the six-beat mantra.

32.

Recitations, rituals, and mantras are merely fabrications.
The single six-beat mantra is the sound of Dharma.
The words you say are nothing but the speech of the
    noble ones.
Knowing that these sounds are empty, chant the six-beat
    mantra.

སྒྲིབ་གཉིས་རྣམ་རྟོག་ཞི་ན་འཁམས་རྟོགས་རྒྱས༎

རང་སྣང་དབང་དུ་འདུས་ན་དགྲ་བགེགས་ཐུལ༎

མཚོག་ཐུན་ཚེ་འདིར་སྐྱལ་མཇྫད་སྲུན་རས་གཟིགས༎

ལས་བཞི་སྒྲུན་གྲུབ་རང་ནས་ཡིག་དྲུག་སྐྲོངས༎

Verses 33–38

Verse 33 is both the conclusion of the short three-verse passage, verses 31–33 to which we just alluded, and the first verse in a longer discussion of practice grounded in nondual awareness. Nondual awareness, Patrul Rinpoche emphasizes, is in turn grounded in the elimination of the two classes of obscurations. The first of these are the affective obscurations. These are the manifestations of attraction and aversion, including greed, lust, anger, and despondency. These obscurations constitute the emotional fog that obscures the true nature of reality.

33.

As the two conceptual obscurations diminish, realization
grows.

As you gain control over appearances, obstacles and foes
are tamed.

In this very life, Avalokiteśvara bestows the high and the
common practices.

Having spontaneously accomplished the four acts, chant
the six-beat mantra.

The second class are the cognitive obscurations, such as the superimposition of intrinsic identity, or the illusion of a self. These obscurations distort
reality by incorrect ideation, either explicit or implicit. Patrul Rinpoche
emphasizes here that both are conceptual (*rnams rtog*)—that our dysfunctional affective states arise from conceptuality as well. In this regard,
he is following Asanga in *Abhisamayālaṃkāra* (*The Ornament of Clear
Realization*).

གང་ཞར་གཏོར་མ་ཞར་གྲོལ་མགྲོན་ལ་བསྔོས།།

སྲུང་སྐྱོང་སྲུ་ཚུ་གང་སྲུང་ས་ལ་འདེབས།།

གཉིས་མེད་ལྷ་ཕྱག་སེམས་ཞིང་མགྲོན་ལས་འཚལ།།

ཚོས་སྐྱོང་ཡོངས་རྫོགས་དང་ནས་ཡིག་དྲུག་སྒྲོངས།།

ཞེ་སྡང་དགྲ་བོ་ཁྱམས་པའི་མཚོན་གྱིས་ཕྱལ།།

རིགས་དྲུག་གཉེན་འཁོར་སྐྱིང་རྗེའི་ཐབས་ཀྱིས་སྐྱོངས།།

དང་པའི་ཞིང་ལ་ནཟམས་རྫོགས་ལོ་ཏོག་རྫོས།།

ཆི་འཇིགས་ལས་རྫོགས་དང་ནས་ཡིག་དྲུག་སྒྲོངས།།

34.

Dedicate whatever arises to the guests of spontaneous
liberation.

Mold whatever appears into the tsa-tsas of empty
appearance.

Offer nondual prostrations to the protector, the nature of
mind.

Performing only virtuous acts, chant the six-beat mantra.

35.

Subdue the enemy of hatred with the sword of love.

Protect the family of the denizens of the six realms with
skillful care.

Reap from the field of confidence the harvest of experience
and realization.

Accomplishing your life's work, chant the six-beat mantra.

བདེན་ཞེན་རོ་རྐན་ཞེན་མེད་མི་ལ་སྐྱེགས།།

འདིར་སྤྱང་བདུན་ཚིགས་སྙིང་པོའི་ཚོས་ཀྱིས་དེད།།

ཚོགས་བསགས་རོ་བཀྲགས་ཚེ་རབས་གསུར་དུ་བསྲོས།།

གཉེན་པོའི་དགེ་རྩོགས་དང་ནས་ཡིག་དྲུག་སྤྲོངས།།

36.

Burn the corpse of attachment to reality in the fire of
nonattachment.

Through the essence of Dharma, conduct the funeral rites
for appearances.

Dedicate the merit you gain from the smoke offering for
their next life.

Having dedicated all of your virtue to these dead, chant
the six-beat mantra.

དད་པའི་བུ་ཚ་ཁམས་ལེན་ཚོས་སྦྱོར་ཆུད། །

འདིར་སྐྱང་ཁྲིམས་དུ་ཞིན་ལོག་བུ་ཐབང་ཞིག །

སྐྱིང་རྗེའི་བུ་མོ་ཁམས་གསུམ་མག་པར་ཁྲིག །

གསོན་པོའི་ཚོས་རྗེ་གས་དང་ནས་ཡིག་དྲུག་སྦྱོང་། །

སྐྱང་ཚད་འཐུལ་པ་ལགས་ཏེ་བརྟེན་པར་མེད། །

འཁོར་འདས་རྣམ་རྟོག་ཚམ་སྟེ་ལོགས་ན་མེད། །

རྣམ་རྟོག་ཕར་གྲོལ་ཤེས་ན་ས་ལམ་རྗོགས། །

གྲོལ་ལུགས་གཉད་ཀྱི་དང་ནས་ཡིག་དྲུག་སྦྱོང་། །

37.

Place your son—confidence—at the Dharma door of
   your practice.
Give the house of appearances to your son-in-law—
   renunciation.
Marry your daughter—care—to the bridegroom of the
   triple world.
Having done your duty to the living, chant the six-beat
   mantra.

38.

All appearance is illusion; there's no truth in it.
Samsara and nirvana are mere conceptions, nothing more.
To know conceptions as instantly liberated is to complete the
   path.
Turning the key to liberation, chant the six-beat mantra.

VERSE 37

The triple world comprises the desire realm, the form realm, and the form-
less realm.

རང་སེམས་རིག་སྟོང་གཉིས་མེད་ཆོས་སྐུའི་རང་།།

མ་བཅོས་གཉུག་མར་བཞག་ན་རང་གསལ་འཆར།།

བྱར་མེད་ཆིག་ཆོད་རང་དུ་གྲུས་ཆོས་ཉིད།།

རིག་སྟོང་རྗེན་པར་ཆོག་ལ་ཡིག་དྲུག་སྒྱུངས།།

VERSES 39–42

Here Patrul Rinpoche further develops the theme of nonduality of subject and object. Mind, he reminds his reader, is primordially nondual: duality is a superimposition on our experience that is not in itself distinguished into subjective and objective poles. Moreover, Patrul Rinpoche emphasizes, following Nāgārjuna, that the two truths are nondually related. To understand the conventional truth completely is to understand its emptiness, and hence to understand the ultimate truth; to understand emptiness is to understand that it is only the emptiness of conventional phenomena, and only dependent origination. Finally, drawing on both

39.

Your mind, nondually aware and empty, is the embodiment
of truth.
So if you leave things in their natural, unfabricated state,
clarity will arise on its own.
Only by doing nothing at all will you do what is to be done.
Letting everything remain in naked, empty awareness, chant
the six-beat mantra.

the Madhyamaka and Yogācāra traditions, Patrul Rinpoche asserts that
to understand the world we experience correctly is to understand that all
appearance is constructed by mind, not as the veridical apprehension of
distinct objects. Moreover, to understand the mind is to understand it
as merely the locus of appearance. This is the key to understanding the
nonduality of subject and object. Patrul Rinpoche refers to the mind
so understood as the ordinary mind (*tha mal sems*). This technical term
denotes not the mind as it ordinarily appears to us but the mind as it
always exists in reality.

གནས་པའི་སྟེང་ནས་འགྱུ་བའི་རྩིས་མ་ཕྱུད་ཚོད་ད།།

འགྱུ་བའི་དང་ནས་གནས་པའི་རང་རོ་སྤྱོས།།

གནས་འགྱུ་གཉིས་མེད་ཐ་མལ་ཤེས་པ་སྐྱོང་ས།།

ཇེ་གཅིག་ཉམས་ཀྱི་དང་ནས་ཡིག་དྲུག་སྒྲོང་ས།།

ཀུན་རྫོབ་བརྟགས་ནས་དོན་དམ་གཏན་ལ་ཕོབ།།

དོན་དམ་དང་ནས་ཀུན་རྫོབ་འཆར་ཚུལ་སྤྱོས།།

བདེན་གཉིས་དབྱེར་མེད་བློ་བྲལ་གཉུག་མའི་གཤིས།།

སྤྲོས་བྲལ་ལྷ་བའི་དང་ནས་ཡིག་དྲུག་སྒྲོང་ས།།

40.

In a moment of stillness, cut through restless pursuit.
See the essence of stillness in that restless movement.
Find the ordinary mind in the nonduality of motion and
  stillness.
Practicing one-pointedness, chant the six-beat mantra.

41.

The ultimate falls out when you investigate the conventional.
And see how the conventional arises from the ultimate!
The two truths are inseparable, transcend thought, natural
  and glorious.
With a view free of fabrication, chant the six-beat mantra.

སྣང་བའི་སྟེང་དུ་སེམས་ཀྱི་ཞེན་པ་ཆོད།།

སེམས་ཀྱི་སྟེང་དུ་སྣང་བའི་རྟེན་ཕུག་རྡིབ།།

སྣང་སེམས་གཉིས་མེད་རྒྱུ་གྲོལ་ཕྱལ་བ་ཆེ།།

རོ་གཅིག་རྟོགས་པའི་དང་ནས་ཡིག་དྲུག་སྦྱོངས།།

42.

Cut off the mind's obsession with appearance.

Let the whole structure of deluded appearance crumble away.

The nonduality of mind and appearance is an infinite
expanse.

Realizing that single essence, chant the six-beat mantra.

VERSE 42

"Single essence" is the translation of the Tibetan *ro gcig*, which itself is the translation of the Sanskrit *eka-rasa*. The root metaphor of *rasa* is the sap of a plant, hence our translation of that term as essence or nature (thus we translate *ro gcig* as "single essence" and *ro snyoms* as "common nature").

ༀ༔

སེམས་ཀྱི་རང་བཞིན་རིག་སྟོང་གཉུག་མར་གྲོལ༔།

རིག་པའི་རང་རྩལ་སེམས་ཆོག་རང་སར་དག༔།

སེམས་རིག་གཉིས་མེད་ཕྱག་ལེ་གཅིག་གི་ངང་༔།

བསྒོམ་མེད་ཆོས་སྐུའི་རང་ནས་ཡིག་དྲུག་སྟོངས༔།

Verses 43–49

While mind (*sems*) and awareness (*rig pa*) are identical in scope in the sense that they are each grounded in nonduality, Patrul Rinpoche is not saying that *sems* and *rig pa* are identical. According to the Dzogchen tradition, one needs to cut through (*khregs chod*) the delusions associated with *sems* in order to experience this primordial awareness (*rig pa*).

The central phrase in these verses is "on the spot" (*rang sar*). Patrul Rinpoche is calling attention here to the fact that liberation is not the result of a process that begins with bondage and that is achieved through transformation, but rather that liberation is the original nature of all phenomena,

43.

The nature of mind is liberated within innate empty
   awareness.

In the spontaneity of awareness, thought is purified on
   the spot.

Mind and awareness are nondual, essentially identical
   in scope.

Embodying the truth without meditating, chant the
   six-beat mantra.

a nature always present but occluded in samsara. It is to be *realized*, not
to be *achieved*. Mind itself is already pure awareness; the manifestation
of mind as distinct from its object is illusory. The objects of the six sense
faculties (the five external faculties and the introspective faculty) are themselves already the bases of liberation if experienced as they are, free from
attachment and aversion and free from dualistic appearance.

In verses 44–49, Patrul Rinpoche explores the way that this liberation on
the spot occurs in the context of well-known Tibetan Buddhist practices,
alternating between those of highly advanced practitioners and ordinary

༺༻

གཟུགས་སྣང་ལྷ་རུ་ཤས་ན་བསྐྱེད་རིམ་གནད།།

མཚན་དང་མི་མཚན་སྣང་ཞེན་རང་སར་གྲོལ།།

ཞེན་མེད་སེམས་ཀྱི་སྣང་ཆ་འཕགས་པའི་སྐུ།།

མཚོང་སྣང་རང་གྲོལ་དང་ནས་ཡིག་དྲུག་སྒྲོངས།།

people. In verses 44 and 46, he addresses the development and completion stages of the graduated path to awakening. The development stages are the early stages of practice in which the practitioner cultivates the skills and virtues necessary for the attainment of higher realizations. In the completion stage, the practitioner attains those insights and realizations. Patrul Rinpoche emphasizes the nonduality of practice and realization, and so of development and completion, a distinctive Dzogchen perspective on the graduated path. In verses 45 and 47 he addresses mantra recitation and prayer. In verses 48 and 49 he considers the outcome of all of these practices, the realization of the common nature of all things (*ro snyoms*).

44.

To know appearance as divine is the point of the development stage.

Clinging to appearance as beautiful or not is liberated on the
spot.

The nonclinging to appearance is the embodiment of the
noble ones.

In the self-liberation of visual appearance, chant the six-beat
mantra.

To say that all things have a common nature is to say that they are all
ultimately empty and conventionally real, and moreover that attributions
of properties such as beautiful or ugly, pleasant or unpleasant, friend or
enemy are reflections of delusion and attachment to appearance, obscur-
ing the single nature of all phenomena. In this discussion Patrul Rinpoche exploits the classification of the different modes of consciousness,
working through all the sensory faculties and finishing with the introspective faculty.

སྨྲ་སྨྲང་ཕྱགས་སུ་ཤེས་ན་བརྒྱས་བརྗོད་གནད།།

སྣན་དང་མི་སྣན་སྨྲང་ཞིན་རང་སར་གྲོལ།།

ཞིན་མེད་འཁོར་འདས་རང་སྒྲ་ཡིག་དྲུག་གསུང་།།

ཐོས་སྨྲང་རང་གྲོལ་དང་ནས་ཡིག་དྲུག་སྒྲོང་།།

དྲི་སྨྲང་སྐྱེ་མེད་ཤེས་ན་ཙོགས་རིམ་གནད།།

ཞིམ་དང་མི་ཞིམ་ཞིན་སྨྲང་རང་སར་གྲོལ།།

ཞིན་མེད་དྲི་སྨྲང་འཕགས་པའི་ཚུལ་ཁྲིམས་དང་།།

དྲི་སྨྲང་རང་གྲོལ་དང་ནས་ཡིག་དྲུག་སྒྲོངས།།

45.

To know the appearance of sound as mantra is the point
of recitation.

Clinging to sound as melodious or not is liberated on
the spot.

Transcending clinging to samsara and nirvana is the very
voice of the six beats.

In the self-liberation of sonic appearance, chant the six-
beat mantra.

46.

To know the appearance of scents as unarisen is the point of
the completion stage.

Clinging to scent as pleasant or not is liberated on the spot.

Transcending clinging to the appearance of scent is the discipline of the noble ones.

In the self-liberation of the fragrant, chant the six-beat
mantra.

རོ་སླུང་ཚོགས་སུ་ཤེས་ན་མཆོད་པའི་གནད། །

བཅུད་དང་མི་བཅུད་ཞིན་སླུང་རང་སར་གྲོལ། །

ཞིན་མེད་བཟའ་བཏུང་འཕགས་པ་དགྱེས་པའི་ རྫས། །

རོ་སླུང་རང་གྲོལ་དང་ནས་ཡིག་དྲུག་སློང་། །

རེག་སླུང་མཉམ་ཞིང་ཤེས་ན་རོ་སྟོ་མས་གནད། །

འགྲང་ལྟོག་ཚ་གྲང་སླུང་བ་རང་སར་གྲོལ། །

ཞིན་མེད་ཕྱི་ནང་རེག་བྱ་ལྷུའི་ཕྲིན་ལས། །

རེག་སླུང་རང་གྲོལ་དང་ནས་ཡིག་དྲུག་སློང་། །

47.

To know the appearance of taste as offering is the point
of worship.

Clinging to taste as delicious or not is liberated on the spot.

Transcending clinging to food and drink is delightful
to the noble ones.

In the self-liberation of taste, chant the six-beat mantra.

48.

To know the equivalence of feelings is the point of
common nature.

The appearance of being full or hungry, hot or cold,
is liberated on the spot.

Transcending clinging to inner and outer feelings is the
activity of the gods.

In the self-liberation of feeling, chant the six-beat mantra.

༤༩

ཆོས་ཀུན་སྟོང་པར་ཤེས་ན་ལྟ་བའི་གནད། །

བདེན་ཧྲུན་བློ་ཡི་འཛིན་སྟངས་རང་སར་གྲོལ། །

ཞེན་མེད་སྣང་སྲིད་འཁོར་འདས་ཆོས་སྐུའི་དང་། །

རྟོག་ཚོགས་རང་གྲོལ་དང་ནས་ཡིག་དྲུག་སྒྲོངས། །

༥༠

ཉེ་སྲུང་ཡུལ་ཇེས་མ་འབྱེད་བློ་བློ་སྟོམས། །

ཁོ་སྲུང་རང་ཆར་རང་གྲོལ་གསལ་སྟོང་དང་། །

གསལ་སྟོང་མི་ལོང་ཡེ་ཤེས་ལོགས་ན་མེད། །

ཉེ་སྲུང་རང་གྲོལ་དང་ནས་ཡིག་དྲུག་སྒྲོངས། །

Verses 50–54

In this set of verses, Patrul Rinpoche urges a redirection of attention in practice from the objects of awareness to awareness itself. When we react in anger or aversion to a person or object, our attention is directed to the

49.

To know the emptiness of all phenomena is the point of the
view.

Belief in truth and falsity is liberated on the spot.

Transcending clinging to experience—whether of samsara or
nirvana—is the vast embodiment of reality.

In the self-liberation of cognition, chant the six-beat mantra.

50.

Don't pursue the object of aversion; attend to the angry
mind.

The appearance of anger instantly self-liberates into radiant
emptiness.

Radiant emptiness is nothing but mirror-like insight.

In the self-liberation of aversion, chant the six-beat mantra.

object of our attitude. The problem, however, is not the object but the attitude itself. Instead of being concerned with the object of our emotion, we
should therefore be concerned with our state of mind. When we are proud,

ང་རྒྱལ་ཡུལ་རྟེས་མ་འཛིན་འཛིན་རྫོ་སློས།།

མཚོག་འཛིན་རང་ཁར་རང་གྲོལ་ཡེ་སྟོང་དང་།།

ཡེ་སྟོང་མཉམ་ཉིད་ཡེ་ཤེས་ལོགས་ན་མེད།།

ང་རྒྱལ་རང་གྲོལ་དང་ནས་ཡིག་དྲུག་སྐོངས།།

we direct our attention to ourselves. We should be concerned instead with eliminating the pride (by attending to the prideful, grasping mind), and eliminating as well, mutatis mutandis, other dysfunctional affective states. Finally, we should be alive to the illusory nature of conceptual thought. Conceptual thought does not deliver the world as it is. Instead it fabricates a world that never could be, and that fabrication is the source of bondage and suffering.

Patrul Rinpoche also notes that each of the relevant dysfunctional psychological states self-liberates into a specific kind of liberative wisdom.

51.

Don't pursue or grasp the object of pride; attend to the
    grasping mind.
Arrogance instantly self-liberates into primordial emptiness.
Primordial emptiness is nothing but insight into the identity
    of all things.
In the self-liberation of pride, chant the six-beat mantra.

Anger becomes mirror-like insight as we attend to ourselves as angry subjects instead of to those at whom we are angry. Arrogance becomes insight
into the identity of all things as we recognize the emptiness of the self we
take to be so superior, and its interdependence with all things. Clinging
becomes discriminative insight once we see that we cling only by virtue of
the delusion that what we cling to has some intrinsic worth. Discrimination is transformed into skillful insight once we understand that the gulf
we apprehended between the conventional and the ultimate is illusory.
Finally, when we understand that everything we ever experience is fabrication, that understanding itself directly transforms that fabrication into
immediate awareness of the expanse of reality (*dharmadhātu, chos dbying*).

༤༢

འདོད་ཆགས་ཡུལ་རྟེས་མ་ཞེན་ཞེན་བློ་སྤོས།།
ཞེན་སྤྱང་རང་ཁར་རང་གྲོལ་བདེ་སྟོང་དང་།།
བདེ་སྟོང་བོར་ཆོག་ཡེ་ཤེས་ལོགས་ན་མེད།།
འདོད་ཆགས་རང་གྲོལ་དང་ནས་ཡིག་དྲུག་སྟོངས།།

༤༣

ཕྲག་དོག་ཡུལ་རྟེས་མ་འབྱང་དཔྱོད་བློ་སྤོས།།
ཆོག་དཔྱོད་རང་ཁར་རང་གྲོལ་བློ་སྟོང་དང་།།
བློ་སྟོང་ཁ་བྱུབ་ཡེ་ཤེས་ལོགས་ན་མེད།།
ཕྲག་དོག་རང་གྲོལ་དང་ནས་ཡིག་དྲུག་སྟོངས།།

52.

Don't pursue or cling to the object of desire; attend to the
    clinging mind.
The appearance of clinging instantly self-liberates into
    the bliss of emptiness.
The bliss of emptiness is nothing but discriminating insight.
In the self-liberation of desire, chant the six-beat mantra.

53.

Don't pursue the object of envy; attend to the discriminating
    mind.
Discrimination instantly self-liberates into the emptiness of
    mind.
Emptiness of mind is nothing but skillful insight.
In the self-liberation of envy, chant the six-beat mantra.

བདི་སྨུག་ཡུལ་ལ་མ་རྟོགས་རང་རོ་སློས།།

རྟོག་ཚོགས་རང་ཁྱར་རང་གྲོལ་རིག་སྟོང་རང་།།

རིག་སྟོང་ཚོས་དབྱིངས་ཡེ་ཤེས་ཡོགས་ན་མེད།།

བདི་སྨུག་རང་གྲོལ་རང་རས་ཡིག་དྲུག་སློང་།།

54.

Don't assume the reality of the objects of ignorance; attend
to their real nature.

The matrix of conceptual thought is instantly liberated as
empty awareness.

Empty awareness is nothing but insight into the expanse of
reality.

In the self-liberation of ignorance, chant the six-beat mantra.

५५

གཟུགས་པུང་ལེ་སྐྱོང་སྐྱེ་མེད་ནམ་མཁའི་རང་།།
སྐྱོང་ཉིད་རིག་པའི་ཐིག་ལེ་སྒྱུན་རས་གཟིགས།།
འཕགས་པ་ནམ་མཁའི་རྒྱལ་པོ་ལྷོགས་ན་མེད།།
སྐྱོང་ཉིད་ལྷ་བའི་རང་ནས་ཡིག་དྲུག་སྐྱོངས།།

In these verses Patrul Rinpoche employs a number of different names of Avalokiteśvara occurring in the Nyingma Avalokiteśvara tantric cycle, using a different name in each verse. In each case, the meaning of the name is used as a basis for the point made in the verse.

In verses 55–59 Patrul Rinpoche turns to the five aggregates, the constituents of the person. This set of verses echoes the *Heart of Wisdom Sūtra* both in its identification of each of the five aggregates (material form, feeling, perception, dispositions, and consciousness) with emptiness and in the foregrounding of Avalokiteśvara in the context of this metaphysical discussion, thus emphasizing the cultivation of care as the foundation of this insight, as well as the development of care as its consequence.

Like the *Heart Sūtra*, Patrul Rinpoche begins with material form and then works through the other aggregates. He next points to the role of feeling—

55.

The aggregate of form is primordially empty and unarisen,
   like space.
Avalokiteśvara is the essence of empty awareness.
He is none other than the noble Ganganaraja.
From within a clear view of emptiness, chant the six-beat
   mantra.

the experience of pleasure or pain—as that which binds us to objects, and to care as that which releases us from those bonds. He then turns to our perception of the world, asserting that taking perception to be veridical is the source of egoism and bondage, and that care allows us to distance ourselves from that illusion. Egoistic intention leads to a cycle of unhappiness; caring intention to liberation.

VERSE 55

Ganganaraja means *monarch of space*. Space is often a metaphor for emptiness; hence the relevance of this name to the understanding of emptiness mentioned in the final line.

ཆོར་བ་ཡུལ་སེམས་གཉིས་སྦྱེལ་འཆིང་བའི་ཞགས།

མཉམ་ཉིད་གཉིས་མེད་རྟོགས་ན་སྤྱན་རས་གཟིགས།

འཕགས་པ་དོན་ཡོད་ཞགས་པ་ལོགས་ན་མེད།

རོ་མཉམ་རྟོགས་པའི་དང་ནས་ཡིག་དྲུག་སྒྲོངས།

56.

Feeling is the noose that binds the mind to its object.
Avalokiteśvara is the realization that they are nondually
  identical.
He is none other than the noble Amoghapaśa.
In the realization of their common nature, chant the six-beat
  mantra.

VERSE 56

Amoghapaśa means *the noble noose*; hence this name is relevant to the idea
of nonduality—of two identities or realities bound together.

༤༧

འདུ་ཤེས་མཚན་མར་འཛིན་པ་འཁྲུལ་པའི་སྐྱོ།།
འགྲོ་ཀུན་སྙིང་རྗེས་འཛིན་ན་སྨྲ་རྣས་གཟིགས།།
འཕགས་མཆོག་འཁོར་བ་དོང་སྤྲུགས་ལོགས་ན་མེད།།
དམིགས་མེད་སྙིང་རྗེའི་རང་ནས་ཡིག་དྲུག་སྐྱོང་ས།།

༤༨

འདུ་བྱེད་འཁོར་བའི་ལས་ཀྱིས་རིགས་དྲུག་འཁོར།།
ཕྱིན་ནི་མཉམ་ཉིད་ཏོགས་ན་སྨྲ་རྣས་གཟིགས།།
འགྲོ་འདུལ་ཕྲུགས་རྗེ་ཆེན་པོ་ལོགས་ན་མེད།།
གཞན་ཕན་པོ་གཅིག་རང་ནས་ཡིག་དྲུག་སྐྱོང་ས།།

VERSE 57

Saṃsāramanthana means *he who churns the depths of samsara.* The name recalls an epithet of Śiva, the Hindu god—Samudramanthan—who churned the depths of the ocean to retrieve the nectar of immortality.

57.

To hold perceptions to reflect reality is delusion.
To hold all beings in universal care is to be Avalokiteśvara.
He is none other than the noble Saṃsāramanthana.
With nonobjectifying care, chant the six-beat mantra.

58.

Intention and action in samsara turn the wheel of being.
To realize the identity of nirvana and samsara is to be
    Avalokiteśvara,
who is none other than the noble Caturbhuja
    Mahākaruṇikā.
For the benefit of others, who have a single essence, chant the
    six-beat mantra.

VERSE 58

Caturbhuja Mahākaruṇikā means *he who tames beings with great compassion.* This name is hence relevant to the motivation to benefit others.

རྣམ་ཤེས་སེམས་ཀྱི་རང་བཞིན་ཚོགས་བརྒྱད་ཆ།།

སེམས་ཉིད་ཆོས་སྐུར་རྟོགས་ན་སྤྲུན་རས་གཟིགས།།

འཕགས་མཆོག་རྒྱལ་བ་རྒྱ་མཚོ་ལྤོགས་ན་མེད།།

རང་སེམས་སངས་རྒྱས་ཤེས་པས་ཡིག་དྲུག་སྟོངས།།

59.

Consciousness—the nature of mind—is eightfold.

To realize the nature of mind as the embodiment of reality is
to be Avalokiteśvara,

who is none other than the noble Jinasagara.

Since your own mind is the wisdom of the buddhas, chant
the six-beat mantra.

Verse 59

Jinasagara means *ocean of the victors*. The ocean is often a metaphor for vast wisdom, with which the mind is identified in the final line of the verse.

Patrul Rinpoche analyzes the aggregate of consciousness through the Yogācāra eightfold analysis introduced by Vasubandhu—the six sensory consciousnesses, self-consciousness, and the foundation consciousness.

ཕུས་སྐྱང་གདོས་བཅས་འཇིན་པ་འཆིང་བའི་ཞུ།།

སྣང་སྟོང་སྐུ་རུ་ཤེས་ན་སྒྱུན་རིས་གཟིགས།།

འཕགས་མཆོག་ཁ་སརཔ་ཏེ་ལོགས་ནས་ན་མེད།།

སྣང་སྟོང་སྐུའ་སྐུའི་ངང་ནས་ཡིག་དྲུག་སྒྲོངས།།

VERSES 60–64

Patrul Rinpoche turns from the five aggregates to the three sources of action—body, speech, and mind. Each of these exists in one way and appears in another. The body appears to be material, whereas it is in fact an empty ground of caring action; speech seems to be mere sound, but it is in fact mantra—the cause of awakening; mind appears to be essentially conceptual and dualistic, but it is in fact primordially nondual and non-conceptual. In sum, we live in a world that is primordially pure but that appears to us always in an illusory form. Our task in practice is not to purify the world but to abandon the illusory superimposition that arises

60.

Taking the appearance of the body to be material leads to
    bondage.
If you know it as divine, as empty appearance, it is
    Avalokiteśvara,
who is none other than noble Khasarpana.
Since your divine body is empty appearance, chant the
    six-beat mantra.

from dysfunctional cognitive and perceptual instincts, and this cognitive
achievement is made possible only through ethical transformation.

VERSE 60

Khasarpana means *he who glides through the air.* It refers to the ability
of the divine body of Avalokiteśvara to move effortlessly through space,
hence its relevance to the cultivation of a divine body in practice.

རྣ་སྒྲུང་བརྗོད་པའི་སྒྲ་ཚིགས་འཁྲུལ་པའི་རྒྱུ།།
བྲགས་སྟོང་སྤྲུགས་སུ་ཤེས་ན་སྤྲུན་རས་གཟིགས།།
འཕགས་མཆོག་སེ་དེ་སྒྲ་ཞེས་ལོགས་ན་མེད།།
སྒྲ་བྲགས་སྤྲགས་སུ་ཤེས་པས་ཡིག་དྲུག་སློངས།།

སེམས་སྒྲུང་བདེན་ཞིན་འཁྲུལ་པ་འབོར་བའི་རྒྱུ།།
རྟོག་བྲལ་གཤིས་ལ་བཞག་ན་སྤྲུན་རས་གཟིགས།།
འཕགས་མཆོག་སེམས་ཉིད་རང་བསོ་ལོགས་ན་མེད།།
སེམས་ཉིད་ཆོས་སྐུའི་རང་ནས་ཡིག་དྲུག་སློངས།།

VERSE 61

Simhanada means *Lion's Roar*, hence the relevance to sound and mantra.

61.

Taking the appearance of sound to be speech leads to
  delusion.
If you know it as mantra, resounding but empty, it is
  Avalokiteśvara,
who is none other than the noble Simhanada.
Knowing sound itself as mantra, chant the six-beat mantra.

62.

Clinging to the appearance of mind as real is the delusion
  that leads to samsara.
Left in its primordial state, free of conception, the mind is
  Avalokiteśvara,
who is none other than the noble Mahāsaṃdhi cittatā.
Since the mind itself is the embodiment of reality, chant
  the six-beat mantra.

Verse 62

Mahāsaṃdhi cittatā means *he whose mind is in repose.* This epithet is hence
connected here to the mind itself as the embodiment of the true nature of
reality, entirely pacified.

སྣང་སྲིད་ཡེ་ནས་དག་པ་ཆོས་སྐུའི་དང་།།

ཆོས་སྐུའི་རང་ཞལ་མཇལ་ན་སྒྱུན་རས་གཟིགས།།

འཕགས་མཆོག་འཇིག་རྟེན་དབང་ཕྱུག་ལོགས་ན་མེད།།

དག་པ་རབ་འབྱམས་རང་ནས་ཡིག་དྲུག་སྒྲོང་།།

སྐུ་གཅིག་རྒྱལ་བ་ཀུན་འདུས་པ་སྒྱུན་རས་གཟིགས།།

སྤྱགས་གཅིག་སྙིང་པོ་ཀུན་འདུས་ཡི་གེ་དྲུག།

ཆོས་གཅིག་བསྐྱེད་རྫོགས་ཀུན་འདུས་ཁྲ་ཆུབ་སེམས།།

གཅིག་ཤེས་ཀུན་གྲོལ་དང་ནས་ཡིག་དྲུག་སྒྲོང་།།

63.

All that appears or exists is the primordially pure
   embodiment of reality.
When the embodiment of reality is confronted directly,
   it is Avalokiteśvara,
who is none other than the noble Lokeśvara.
From the vast pure expanse, chant the six-beat mantra.

64.

One deity—Avalokiteśvara—embodies all the buddhas.
One mantra—the six beats—is the essence of all mantras.
One Dharma—bodhicitta—comprises all practices from
   development to completion.
Since knowing one liberates all, chant the six-beat mantra.

VERSE 63

Lokeśvara means *lord of the universe.* The name is used here to invoke the
expansiveness of mind achieved in practice and the universal scope of
bodhicitta.

༸༤

བྱས་པས་ཅི་བྱ་བྱ་བྱེད་འབོར་བའི་རྒྱུ།།

བྱས་ཆད་སྐྱིང་པོ་མེད་པའི་ཆུལ་ལ་ལྟོས།།

དངེ་བྱར་མེད་དང་ལ་བཟས་ན་དགའ།།

བྱ་བྱེད་ཆམས་སེ་ཆོག་ལ་ཡིག་དྲུག་སྟོང་ས།།

༸༦

སྨྲས་པས་ཅི་བྱ་སྨྲས་ཆད་བྱེ་མོའི་གཏམ།།

འབྱེལ་མེད་རྣམ་གཡེང་སྐྱེད་པའི་ཆུལ་ལ་ལྟོས།།

དངེ་བརྗོད་མེད་དང་ལ་གནས་ན་དགའ།།

སྨྲ་བརྗོད་ཆད་ཀྱིས་ཆོད་ལ་ཡིག་དྲུག་སྟོང་ས།།

65.

What has all you've done accomplished? It just leads to
  samsara.
Since you can see that it is all so meaningless,
from now on, please just stop acting this way!
Dropping all activities, chant the six-beat mantra.

66.

What have all your words accomplished? They are all just
  idle chatter.
Since you can see that they have caused so much pointless
  distraction,
from now on, please just stop talking this way!
Giving up all speech, chant the six-beat mantra.

སྟོང་བས་ཅི་བྱ་འགྲོ་འདུག་ངལ་བའི་རྒྱུ།།

འཁྱམས་ཞིང་ཚོས་ལས་རིང་བའི་ཚུལ་ལ་ལྟོས།།

ད་ནི་གཅིག་ཏུ་སེམས་བག་ཕབ་ན་དགའ།།

བག་ཡོད་སྟོང་ཀྱིས་སྟོང་ལ་ཡིག་དྲུག་སྒྲོང་།།

ཚོས་པས་ཅི་བྱ་ཚོས་ཆད་མི་གཏང་རྒྱུ།།

ཟ་འདོད་ཚོམ་པ་མེད་པའི་ཚུལ་ལ་ལྟོས།།

ད་ནི་ཏིང་འཛིན་ཟས་སུ་ཟོས་ན་དགའ།།

བཟའ་བཏུང་བྱེད་འཕྲོ་བོར་ལ་ཡིག་དྲུག་སྒྲོང་།།

67.

What has all your traveling accomplished? It just wears
   you out.
Since you can see that your rambling mind has taken you
   so far from the Dharma,
from now on, please let your mind relax in a single place!
At rest, relaxed and at ease, chant the six-beat mantra.

68.

What has all your eating accomplished? It just produces shit.
Since you can see that your appetite is so insatiable,
from now on, please take nourishment from meditation!
Instead of eating and drinking, chant the six-beat mantra.

བསམ་པས་ཅི་བྱ་བསམ་ཚད་འབྲུལ་བའི་ཀླུ། །

བསམ་དོན་ཐོག་ཏུ་མི་ཤིལ་ཆུལ་ལ་སྨོས། །

ད་ནི་ཆེ་འདིའི་བློ་སྣ་བསྡངས་ན་དགའ། །

བློ་ཕག་རང་གིས་ཆོལ་ཡིག་དྲག་སྦྱོངས། །

འཕྲོར་པས་ཅི་བྱ་ལོངས་སྤྱོད་ཞེན་པའི་བློ། །

བསགས་ཚད་ཕུལ་དུ་ལུས་པའི་ཆུལ་ལ་སྨོས། །

ད་ནི་བདག་འཇིན་ཞེན་པ་བཅད་ན་དགའ། །

གསོག་འཇོག་ཆུལ་སྤུབ་པོར་ལ་ཡིག་དྲག་སྦྱོངས། །

69.

What has all your thinking accomplished? It has only
   caused delusion.
Since you can see that you have accomplished so little,
from now on, please don't plan for this life!
Cutting off all thought, chant the six-beat mantra.

70.

What have all your riches accomplished? They just cause
   clinging.
Since you will have to leave it all behind so soon,
from now on, please give up your self-obsession!
Abandoning the pursuit of wealth, chant the six-beat
   mantra.

༧༡

ཧྭལ་བས་ཅི་བྱ་གཞིད་ཆད་གཏི་མུག་དང་།།
སོས་དལ་མི་ཚེ་འཇང་བའི་ཆུལ་ལ་ལྟོས།།
ད་ནི་སྙིང་ནས་བརྩོན་འགྲུས་བསྐྱེད་ན་དགའ།།
ཞིན་མཚན་རྣམ་ག་ཡེང་སྤང་ནས་ཡིག་དྲུག་སྟོང་།།

༧༢

ཕོང་མེད་ཕོང་མེད་སྟོང་པའི་ཕོང་མི་འདུག།
འཆི་བདག་སྒྲོ་བྱུར་སྙིབ་ན་ཅི་ཞིག་བྱ།།
ད་ནི་འཕྲལ་ལ་ལྷུ་ཚོས་འགྲུབ་ན་དགའ།།
ད་ལྟ་ལ་འུར་ཞིད་ཏུ་ཡིག་དྲུག་སྟོང་།།

71.

What has all your sleeping accomplished? You just spend
 your life in a fog.
Since you can see how little time you have left to lie around,
from now on, please start putting in wholehearted effort!
Day and night, ignoring all distraction, chant the six-beat
 mantra.

72.

There's no time! No time! No time to spare!
When the Lord of Death suddenly arrives, what can you do?
Right now, and from now on, please practice the divine
 Dharma.
Right now, with haste, chant the six-beat mantra.

ལོ་དང་ཟླ་གྲངས་ཞག་གི་ཚིས་ཀྱིས་ཅི།།

ད་ལྟ་སྐད་ཅིག་འགྱུར་བའི་ཚུལ་ལ་སློས།།

སྐད་ཅིག་རེ་རེར་སོང་བཞིན་འཆི་ལ་ཉེ།།

ད་ལྟ་ད་ལྟ་ཉིད་ནས་ཡིག་དྲུག་སྒྲོངས།།

ཚོ་ནི་ཉི་མ་བཞིན་དུ་ཕར་ཕར་འགྲོ།།

འཆི་བདག་གྲིབ་སོ་བཞིན་དུ་ཚུར་ཚུར་འོང་།།

ད་ནི་ཚོ་ལྷག་ཉི་ནུས་གྲིབ་སོ་ཙམ།།

སློང་བའི་ལོང་ཙོམ་མི་འདུག་ཡིག་དྲུག་སྒྲོངས།།

73.

How can you count the years, months, and days?
You can see right now that everything changes
      from moment to moment;
So, every passing moment brings you closer to death!
Right now, at this moment, chant the six-beat mantra.

74.

Your life departs like the setting sun.
Death creeps ever closer like the evening shadows.
Even now, your life is just like those fading shadows.
There's no time to waste—chant the six-beat mantra.

༧༥

ཚོས་སུ་ཡི་གེ་དྲུག་པ་བཟང་པོད་དེ།།
ཁ་ཡིངས་མིག་ཡེངས་བརྫུས་པས་འཕུས་མི་འཕྱིན།།
དག་བརྫུས་གྲངས་ལ་ཞེན་པ་ལ་འཕས་སྐྲོ།།
ཅི་གཅིག་སེམས་ལ་སྐྱོས་ལ་ཡིག་དྲུག་སྐྱོངས།།

༧༦

ཡང་དང་ཡང་དུ་རང་གི་སེམས་བརྟགས་ན།།
ཅི་སྤྱར་བྱས་ཀྱང་ཡང་དག་ལམ་ལ་འགྲོ།།
གདམས་པའི་གནད་བརྒྱ་འདུས་པ་འདི་ཉོ་ན།།
གནད་དོན་གཅིག་ལ་སྐྱིལ་ལ་ཡིག་དྲུག་སྐྱོངས།།

VERSE 76

In this verse Patrul Rinpoche is drawing together the points he has made
in the previous discussion. He has advised his reader in verses 44–54 to
attend not to the object of awareness but to the subject, the mind itself—if
one wants to understand and transform the nature of one's experience. In
verses 55–64, he has emphasized the illusory nature of appearance and the

75.

Although the mantra is a fine Dharma practice,

chanting it while gossiping or looking around is fruitless.

To fixate on the number of recitations is to obsess on the
wrong thing.

Focusing single-pointedly on your mind, chant the
six-beat mantra.

76.

If you examine your mind continuously,

whatever you do, you are following the perfect path.

Of the hundreds of essential instructions, this is the
real one.

Uniting all of them into this essential point, chant the
six-beat mantra.

capacity of the mind to see reality correctly. In verses 65–71, he provides specific advice for the transformation of mind. Here he draws that advice together, reminding the reader that it is always most important to attend and transform the subject and not the object of awareness. We might say that the true meaning of *mind only* is that the mind is the only thing you need to worry about and the only thing you can transform.

དང་པོར་སྐྱེས་པའི་སྐྱོན་ལ་སྐྱོ་བའི་གཏམ།།

གཏམ་འདི་རང་གིས་རང་ལ་གདམས་པ་སྟེ།།

རང་བློ་གཏིང་ནས་འགྱུར་བའི་སྙེ་ཕྲུགས་ཚིག།

ཁྱེད་ལ་འབང་འདུའམ་སྣམ་ནས་ཕུལ་བ་ལགས།།

མི་འདུ་ལྟ་སྟོམ་མཐོན་པོའི་གདེངས་ཚད་དང་།།

ཕུགས་གཞིས་བྱ་བཤག་འགྱུབ་པའི་རྣམ་དཔྱོད་བློ།།

རང་གཞན་བློ་གཏད་ཡེར་བའི་འདུན་གྲོས་ཧོམས།།

ཁྱེད་ལ་ཡོད་པར་གྱུར་ན་མཐོལ་ལོ་བཤགས།།

77.

When first I spoke in sadness of the deeds of this impure age,
I intended this talk only for myself.
But since this lament has affected me so deeply,
thinking you might take it the same way, I now offer it to you.

78.

If, unlike me, you are sure of the depth of your view and
    meditation,
and of your understanding of the union of the spiritual and
    the mundane,
and if you are ready to solve your own problems and those
    of others—
I am sorry to have bothered you with all of this.

Verses 77–82

In this conclusion, Patrul Rinpoche sums up the structure of the poem,
beginning with the argument for the abandonment of samsara (verses
5–21), continuing with the articulation of the Madhyamaka view and the
bodhisattva path (verses 22–64), and concluding with an admonition to
practice (verses 65–76).

༡༠

བར་དུ་ལྷུ་སྟོམ་གཏན་ལ་འབེབས་པའི་གཏམ།།

ཆོ་གས་པའི་ཉམས་སྐྱོང་བདག་ལ་མེད་མོད་ཀྱང་།།

ཀུན་མཁྱེན་ཡབ་སྲས་བརྒྱུད་པ་རིན་པོ་ཆེའི།།

གསུང་གིས་བསྐུལ་བའི་གོ་ཡུལ་བཏད་པ་ལགས།།

༡༠

ཐབ་མ་རེས་འབྱུང་ཚོས་ལ་སྐྱལ་བའི་གཏམ།།

གཏམ་འདི་བརྫོད་དོན་མེད་ཀྱང་ཕུགས་ཀྱིས་ཐལ།།

དོན་ཀྱང་སྲས་བཅས་རྒྱལ་བའི་བཞེད་གཞུང་དང་།།

མི་འགལ་ཉམས་སུ་བླངས་ན་སྐུ་དྲིན་ཆེ།།

114

79.

Next, I presented the discourse explaining the view and
meditation.
Although I have no experience of realization,
I just presented the cherished knowledge I gained through
the teachings
of the precious lineage of the omniscient fathers and sons.

80.

Finally, I urged you toward the Dharma.
Although I didn't mean to say all of this, it just burst forth
on its own.
Since it doesn't contradict the teachings of the great masters,
it might be a good idea for you to practice in this way.

དེ་ལྟར་ཐོག་མཐའ་བར་དུ་དགེ་བའི་གཏམ།།

ཐུབ་དགར་ཙེ་རྒྱལ་གྲུབ་པའི་ཐུབ་ཕུག་ཏུ།།

ལྷར་འཛིན་གྲོགས་ཀྱིས་བསྐུལ་བ་མ་བཟོད་ནས།།

དུག་ལྷ་མེ་འབར་ཨ་བུ་རྒྱལ་པོས་བྲིས།།

ཁ་བ་གདུང་རྒྱུང་པར་སོང་ཡང་ཙི་ཚ་སྟེ།།

དོན་བཟང་འཕྲུལ་པ་མེད་པའི་དགེ་ཚོགས་རྒྱུན།།

ཉེད་དང་བདག་བཅས་ཁམས་གསུམ་འགྲོ་བ་ཀུན།།

ཚོས་མཐུན་བསམ་པ་འགྲུབ་པའི་རྒྱུ་ར་བསྒྱོ།།   །དགེའོ།།   །།

81.

These verses, virtuous in the beginning, middle, and end,
were composed by your good-for-nothing uncle, aflame with
    the five poisons,
in response to the pleas of his old friend
in White Cliff Victory Mountain Cave.

82.

This may all be just idle talk, but so what?
The intention is good; it is nondeceptive and leads to virtue.
I dedicate this to the fulfillment of all of our wishes
    that agree with the Dharma
and to all of us in the three worlds!

VERSE 81

The five poisons are primal confusion, attraction, aversion, pride, and envy.

About the Translators

JAY L. GARFIELD is Doris Silbert Professor in the Humanities and professor of philosophy, logic, and Buddhist studies at Smith College and Harvard Divinity School, and professor of philosophy at the University of Melbourne and Central University of Tibetan Studies. His work addresses topics in cognitive science, the philosophy of mind, Buddhist philosophy, and cross-cultural interpretation. Professor Garfield has worked extensively with Tibetan scholars at the Central University of Tibetan Studies and the Institute of Buddhist Dialectics and is the founding director of the Five College Tibetan Studies in India Program, the oldest academic exchange program linking the Tibetan academic community to the Western academic community.

EMILY MCRAE is assistant professor of philosophy at the University of New Mexico. Her work addresses topics in Buddhist ethics, moral psychology, and feminist philosophy. She has studied Tibetan language and Buddhist philosophy at the University of Wisconsin and Rangjung Yeshe Institute in Kathmandu, Nepal.

*Also Available
from Wisdom Publications*

Düdjom Lingpa's Visions of the Great Perfection
Translated by B. Alan Wallace
Foreword by Sogyal Rinpoche

"These texts present the essential meaning of the Great Perfection with great clarity and precision."—Tsoknyi Rinpoche

Buddhahood in This Life
The Great Commentary by Vimalamitra
Translated by Malcolm Smith
Foreword by Chökyi Nyima Rinpoche

"An inspired translation of one of the classics of the Great Perfection, unveiling the extraordinary tradition of the 8th-century pandit Vimalamitra. This book introduces the reader to the secret visionary instructions of Thogal practice, the core of Dzogchen itself. Extensively based on the corpus of the *Seventeen Tantras*, the text reveals the entire Path of the Great Perfection in a fluid and inspiring style which carefully follows the original."
—Jean-Luc Achard, author of *The Six Lamps*

A Gathering of Brilliant Moons
Practice Advice from the Rimé Masters of Tibet
Edited by Holly Gayley and Joshua Schapiro

Deepen your meditation with advice on Buddhist practice from celebrated masters of Tibet's nonsectarian rimé tradition.

Hermit of Go Cliffs
Timeless Instructions from a Tibetan Mystic
Translated and introduced by Cyrus Stearns

"A masterly and evocative translation."—*The Tibet Journal*

Practical Ethics and Profound Emptiness
A Commentary on Nagarjuna's Precious Garland
Khensur Jampa Tegchok
Edited by Thubten Chodron

"We are fortunate to have such important and instructive texts as *Nagarjuna's Precious Garland*, which is here profoundly explained by the eminent scholar Khensur Jampa Tegchok. The world has never been more in need of ethics and wisdom, so this timely book is highly recommended for all who seek authoritative guidance on the Mahayana path."
—Jetsunma Tenzin Palmo, author of *Into the Heart of Life*

Approaching the Great Perfection
Simultaneous and Gradual Methods of Dzogchen Practice in the Longchen Nyingtig
Sam Van Schaik

"An important work for its breadth and attention to detail, this book contains translations of ten texts from the widely practiced treasure cycle called the *Longchen Nyingtig*, as well as a survey of Nyingma history and Jigme Lingpa's corpus. Van Schaik's lucid explanation of the issues and technical vocabulary in the 'seminal heart', or *nyingtig*, teachings provide the reader with an essential framework for tackling the extensive primary source material found in this work."
—*Buddhadharma*

Illuminating the Thirty-seven Practices of a Bodhisattva
Chökyi Dragpa
Translated by Heidi I. Koppl
Introduced by Chökyi Nyima Rinpoche

"*The Thirty-Seven Practices of Bodhisattvas*, composed by the illustrious spiritual master Gyalse Togme, presents profound instructions meant for practical application. The lucid and highly readable commentary by Chökyi Dragpa reveals, with utter clarity, the unity of wisdom and compassion that is at the very heart of the Great Vehicle."—Chökyi Nyima Rinpoche, from the introduction

Approaching the Great Perfection
Simultaneous and Gradual Methods of Dzogchen Practice in the Longchen Nyingtig
Sam Van Schaik

"An important work for its breadth and attention to detail, this book contains translations of ten texts from the widely practiced treasure cycle called the *Longchen Nyingtig*, as well as a survey of Nyingma history and Jigme Lingpa's corpus. Van Schaik's lucid explanation of the issues and technical vocabulary in the 'seminal heart', or *nyingtig*, teachings provide the reader with an essential framework for tackling the extensive primary source material found in this work."
—*Buddhadharma*

Illuminating the Thirty-Seven Practices of a Bodhisattva
Chökyi Dragpa
Translated by Heidi I. Koppl
Introduced by Chökyi Nyima Rinpoche

"*The Thirty-Seven Practices of Bodhisattvas*, composed by the illustrious spiritual master Gyalse Togme, presents profound instructions meant for practical application. The lucid and highly readable commentary by Chökyi Dragpa reveals, with utter clarity, the unity of wisdom and compassion that is at the very heart of the Great Vehicle."—Chökyi Nyima Rinpoche, from the introduction

About Wisdom Publications

Wisdom Publications is the leading publisher of classic and contemporary Buddhist books and practical works on mindfulness. To learn more about us or to explore our other books, please visit our website at wisdompubs.org or contact us at the address below.

Wisdom Publications
199 Elm Street
Somerville, MA 02144 USA

We are a 501(c)(3) organization, and donations in support of our mission are tax deductible.

Wisdom Publications is affiliated with the Foundation for the Preservation of the Mahayana Tradition (FPMT).